CHANGING LANES

Advance Praise

"We as entrepreneurs build a business to have control so we can to do the things we love. Unfortunately, after so much hard work and sacrifice, business owners realize the limited control they have over their outcome when they go to market without a plan. Sara and her story provide an amazing example of how owners can regain the control they always wanted and create a successful exit that has many options! The goal is freedom and happiness. *Changing Lanes* is a must-have resource for the journey!

—**Ryan Tansom**, President, Solidity Financial

"Passion, vision and emotion are important elements in building successful businesses, particularly family businesses. In this engaging business novella, Gina Catalano provides business owners with invaluable insights into how to deal with these important elements to successfully transition from their business. Gina's carefully structured and beautifully written book is a significant contribution to the body of work on business exits and transitions."

—**Geoff Green**, founder of GRG Momentum and author of *The Smart Business Exit*

"One of the biggest challenges I've had in growing my business is making sure it stays organized. I'm continually restructuring and redefining workflows, policies, and procedures. When I first started, I made the major mistake of not working on an exit strategy. I was entertained by the story and learned a lot from the experience. If you don't want to liquidate your business when you are ready for the next great endeavor in your life, you

MUST read *Changing Lanes* to learn how you can exit your company successfully: to either hand it off to your family or sell it so you can enjoy the life you've always wanted."

—**Jaime Jay**, Owner, Slapshot Studio

"As she did in *Tandem Leadership: How Your #2 Can Make You #1,* in *Changing Lanes,* Gina Catalano shows you how having a strong team in place can make you and your business more successful. With the help of a mentor, our fictional heroine, Sara Berry, is ready to sell her business but is disappointed to find out that her business isn't quite worth what she had hoped. With the guidance from a mentor and a renewed passion for her business and her life, Sara is able to successfully ready herself for the future. From my own perspective as a CFO and entrepreneur, Sara's story carves an actionable path to the most hassle-free migration to the owners' realization of the highest value for her business."

—**Pam Prior**, CEO, Priorities Group Inc.
and best-selling author of *Your First CFO*

"Having spent 25+ years in the consulting and coaching business, I have witnessed firsthand that most business owners don't know what they don't know when it comes to selling or succeeding their business. Remarkably, Gina Catalano has written a book that will appeal to most owners trying to decide when and how to sell. Her unique writing style masterfully weaves a compelling story to simplify the process, helping them to effectively plan for their future. A quick read that checks all the subjects boxes in a sometimes-misunderstood process."

—**Nigel K. Moore**, President & CEO,
Total Wellness Strategies, LLC

"Every entrepreneur will benefit from reading this book! It's perfectly written and illustrates the problems and challenges entrepreneurs likely have in their business – especially the ones they are not able to see yet. Every entrepreneur can benefit from riding alongside Sara, the main character, on her journey to discover what is next and uncover what has been missing that has left her feeling uninspired by the dream she worked so hard to create. The story perfectly shows how not being prepared for selling your business can have a detrimental impact not only on the money you walk away with but also on your happiness. The guiding questions at the end of each chapter give the reader a way to easily reflect on their own business."

—**Cassie Parks**, Business Coach and best-selling author of *Manifest $10,000* and *Double Your Business*

"Gina Catalano has done a superb job in *Changing Lanes* at providing superb value for businesses to better plan and execute their long-term vision and business exit strategy. This hands-on framework will clearly help owners and business leaders achieve stronger results with a clearer roadmap that includes specific tools to help make it happen. If we could simply re-set America's businesses to start with the end in mind, the economy would gain enormous new prosperity and productivity while the value of individual businesses would sky-rocket, especially at that most critical moment of eventual business exits.

—**Alex Rodriguez**, Vice President,
Arizona Technology Council

CHANGING LANES

The Owner's Guide to A Successful Exit

GINA CATALANO

NEW YORK

NASHVILLE • MELBOURNE • VANCOUVER

CHANGING LANES
The Owner's Guide to A Successful Exit

Published in New York, New York, by Morgan James Publishing in partnership with Difference Press. Morgan James is a trademark of Morgan James, LLC. www.MorganJamesPublishing.com

The Morgan James Speakers Group can bring authors to your live event. For more information or to book an event visit The Morgan James Speakers Group at www.TheMorganJamesSpeakersGroup.com.

ISBN 978-1-68350-631-7 paperback
ISBN 978-1-68350-632-4 eBook
Library of Congress Control Number: 2017909536

Cover Design by:
Chris Treccani
www.3dogdesign.net

Interior Design by:
Bonnie Bushman
The Whole Caboodle Graphic Design

In an effort to support local communities, raise awareness and funds, Morgan James Publishing donates a percentage of all book sales for the life of each book to Habitat for Humanity Peninsula and Greater Williamsburg.

Get involved today! Visit
www.MorganJamesBuilds.com

TABLE OF CONTENTS

INTRODUCTION

When I wrote my last book, *Tandem Leadership: How Your #2 Can Make You #1,* it was with the intention to help entrepreneurs and business owners be more successful in adding that first "#2" or "second-in-command" to their team. Successfully adding that first key person to share the journey is pivotal, and the impact will be felt for years to come. At the beginning of your business you may need someone to help you deal with the daily challenges of a start-up, someone who shares the will to succeed and enjoys the thrill of navigating uncharted waters. It is often at this crossroads that we have to confront our own weaknesses and understand that it is no longer advantageous to us or our businesses to go it alone. Implemented correctly, an intentional strategy of opening our businesses to the right

#2 adds momentum that moves us more quickly toward our chosen destination.

While *Tandem Leadership* focused on the early stages of an entrepreneur's journey, the experience of hitting a wall (or reaching a plateau) and the need to make executive team changes repeats itself throughout the lifecycle of a business. I was surprised by the number of seasoned business owners who found the *Tandem Leadership* model helpful, even though they were well past their own business start-up. For some it was remembering the fits and starts of finding the right pairing, and for others it was the pain of knowing that the person who helped them achieve their current success was no longer suited to continue on the rest of the journey. But one thing stood out to these journeyman entrepreneurs: they had an eye to the future and were looking for someone to accompany them through the last phase of business ownership – successfully preparing the business for sale or transition to the next generation.

Many of the sensationally successful entrepreneurial stories we read and hear about focus on a whiz kid with an idea, technology, or an app that launches a business to a multimillion- (or even multibillion) dollar valuation in seemingly a few short years. Indeed, the fantastic success of Mark Zuckerberg (Facebook), Tony Hsieh (Zappos), and Sara Blakely (Spanx), just to name a few, make this seem like the norm rather than the exception. It might surprise you to learn that the average age of US business owners is actually 50.7 years old. Indeed, our "average business owner" could easily be the parent of the under-30 founders of tech darlings such as Snapchat and Stripe whose combined net worth is near $10 billion dollars!

Bo Burlingham reminds us in his book, *Finish Big,* "sooner or later, all entrepreneurs leave their businesses, and all businesses are sold, given away, or liquidated." In *Changing Lanes* we meet our fictional hero, Sara Berry. Successful by the most basic business measures – great products, a profitable business, loyal customers and employees – she has owned her business for nearly 20 years. Having faced some recent personal and professional challenges, she realizes that what got her to this point in her business may not help her to the finish in the way she intended. With the help of Bill McEntire from *Tandem Leadership,* Sara is able to clarify her challenges and identify the opportunities before her. Knowing that Sara will need to consider a company future that does not include her at the helm, she and Bill craft a plan to help Sara ensure a return on investment for her life's work as well as assure her a meaningful life beyond her business.

Ultimately, "entrepreneur" is code for "freedom." Enjoying your business and your life, being able to sell your business when and to whom you'd like for the amount you dream of – all represent the ultimate freedom for most owners. Whether you're at the beginning of your entrepreneurial journey or nearing the finish, I hope Sara's story and *Changing Lanes* will give you a blueprint for your own "freedom path." After all, when you started your business you had big dreams. Why should the finish be any different?

CHAPTER 1

Sara Berry pulled into her parking space. She let out an audible sigh.

She looked up at the historical building that housed her company – BabyBerry – and remembered the first time she saw it. Her realtor, claiming she had found the "perfect" place for Sara's growing company, urged her to look at the space. After five years, BabyBerry had outgrown Sara's basement and kitchen table, and it was time to find a proper space. The original tenants – Stone & Sons Trunks (for "Ladies Fine Garments") – had left years ago, and the building had endured several reincarnations after the need for steamer trunks had passed. But on that first day Sara could see the potential and fell in love with the old brick building. She thought it the perfect place for her and her small team to make her now-coveted BabyBerry totes and diaper bags. The then-current tenants were moving out to one of the new industrial parks on the outskirts of town, and so she signed the lease without a second thought. Ten years later, BabyBerry had grown as expected, and Sara had seized the opportunity to buy the building. During that decade, the industrial tone of the area had changed and Sara loved the funky coffee shops, cafes, and boutiques that had sprung up around BabyBerry.

It was Monday. This morning, as they had done for the past 15 years, the BabyBerry team would hold "the Weekly," where Sara's 40-person company would look at the production and sales numbers as well as any customer complaints or problems. While the business had always had been profitable, sales had recently flattened. The Monday meetings had become less enjoyable. She took a deep breath and said to no one in particular, "You can do this!"

The meeting started promptly at 9:00 a.m. in their large conference room. As usual, Carol Ann, the Production Supervisor, ran through the production numbers. Darren, the Sales and Marketing Director, read a letter from a customer that had come in via the website over the weekend.

Dear BabyBerry Team,

I am 20 years old and will be having my first baby (a little girl – I'm so excited!!!). Last week I had my baby shower and my two best friends went in together to give me your Emily bag that I wanted. I found out later that my mom also had one of the very first BabyBerry bags when

I was born. I've attached two pix for you to see. One is of my Mom holding me when I was about six months old with her BabyBerry bag! The other one is of my mom and me now with my BabyBerry bag! My mom said hers was a real lifesaver. I can't wait to use mine after my little girl arrives next month.

Thank you for making such a good product!

Kelsey St. James

P.S. My mom said she wished she had kept her original BabyBerry bag, but she gave it to a cousin to use after she didn't need it anymore.

Darren passed the email with the pictures around so that everyone could see them. All of the BabyBerry bags had a small embossed leather tag sewn inside stamped with the year it was manufactured, the style, and the sewer's, or "crafter's," name. Two of the original employees were still working at BabyBerry – Carol Ann and Consuela. They tried to determine from the photo which bag it was and who had made it.

"I'm not sure, but I bet that's one of the first bags that Kit made," Carol Ann said. "Does the woman look familiar to you at all? Didn't you only sell to people you knew in the beginning?"

Sara picked up the photo. She didn't recognize the woman at all. "Probably a daughter of a friend of a friend. What a small world!"

She asked Darren to send her a copy of the email and get a release from Kelsey St. James and her mother so her email could be posted on the website. In the beginning, BabyBerry had been fortunate with product placement in some higher-end children's boutiques as well as several regional department store chains that had a strong emphasis on children's clothing. Understanding that working parents were using the Internet more, they had decided to invest in an online store and that had paid off. Telling the BabyBerry story and creating a whole BabyBerry online world had been well received by the customers and retailers alike. BabyBerry wasn't a large company, but it had developed a cult following with its little bag. Kelsey St. James would become their next feature on BabyBerry.com.

Returning to her office, Sara looked at the photo again and was thrown back in time. *I easily could have been the woman holding little baby Kelsey*, she thought.

While Sara was the company founder, it was her mother, Kit, who had given Sara the idea to start her company. As a young mother with a two-year-old daughter and newborn twin sons, Sara found herself overwhelmed by her trio of children under three. Going anywhere with all of them was an adventure, to say the least, and Kit did everything she could to help her only daughter. Noticing the typical diaper bags weren't working all that well for Sara, Kit created a tote bag that was both extremely functional and easy to carry. And it didn't look like a diaper bag! After more than one of Sara's friends (or Kit's friends who wanted one for their daughters) asked to have one made, they both realized that they were onto something. BabyBerry was born.

In some ways, it seemed like yesterday. But the age of her children told a different tale. Eliza was 22 and would graduate this spring, while Trevor and Matt were now almost 20. Sara couldn't believe how the years had flown by!

She wished she could ask Kit if she recognized the woman in the photo. But she couldn't.

A little over a year ago, a brain aneurism, swiftly and without warning, had taken her mother's life. Sara's father had found her and called the ambulance while Sara raced to the hospital to meet them. As soon as she saw her father, Sara knew. Kit was gone. Sara missed her every day, but even more acutely on days like today when she wanted to ask her a question or seek her advice.

Kelsey St. James' mother wasn't the only question on Sara's mind. She picked up the letter she had received on Friday and had set aside because she wanted to read it again with a fresh perspective on Monday morning.

Dear Ms. Berry:

Our firm, Pine River Group, has been retained on behalf of an interested party to purchase BabyBerry, and I would like to discuss this with you as soon as possible. I understand you may have received inquiries in the past, but rest assured this is a fully qualified offer and will be well worth your time to explore.

Please contact me at the information above at your earliest convenience.

Sincerely,
D. Michael Harris, Senior Partner

D. Michael Harris was correct. She had received letters of inquiries before. Most of them had ended up in the trash, because BabyBerry wasn't for sale. Still, she brought the letter home over the weekend and reviewed it with her husband, Tom. Tom had a small real estate law practice, and while mergers and acquisitions wasn't his area of expertise, he had promised to contact someone he knew on Monday to do some digging for her.

The phone rang and interrupted her thoughts. It was Tom.

"Hey babe, I was hoping to ask you to lunch today, but it looks like I'm going to need to sit in on a call. Do you have a few minutes to go over what I have about the M&A guys?"

"We just finished up the Weekly. This works fine. Anything new?"

"Well, a little. I spoke with Brad Thompson," he told her. "He said Pine River has a decent reputation. Most likely this is more than just a fishing expedition, but they're probably trolling some of your competitors too. He said he knew some people to talk to and would get back to me by tomorrow."

"Interesting," she said. "So, this might be tied to a real offer?"

"It could be. You know, Sara, you've worked really hard all these years," Tom said. "Maybe it *is* time to think about selling."

"Maybe, but…." Before Sara could finish she could hear someone talking to Tom.

He interrupted her. "Sara, my call is starting now. Brad said that you could give him a call directly if you wanted to. I emailed you his info."

She squeezed in a "thanks" and "love you" before Tom hung up.

She checked the clock. Sara had a meeting with Lydia, BabyBerry's Design and Product Director, at 2:00 p.m., and she needed to grab lunch. When they first moved into this building, she had to drive to pick up lunch. But now the town's old secondhand stores and insurance storefronts had given way to trendy boutiques and quirky cafes. There were plenty of options to choose from.

She told her assistant, Char, that she was leaving. Char said, "Sara, I'd be happy to order lunch for you."

"Thanks, but I need to stretch my legs and get some fresh air," she said as she walked out the door.

Sara started down toward the new salad restaurant and then promptly walked right past. It was definitely a burger-and-fries kind of day, and she knew exactly where she wanted to go. Jerry's Top Town Diner had not only survived the town's gentrification, but thrived. Apparently nostalgia – not to mention good, old-fashioned diner food – made for good business. She and Tom didn't go there as often now that their children were away at school, and avoided it on weekends when the lines were out the door.

She found her way up to the counter. As she was getting ready to sit down, she heard a familiar voice bellow, "Sara Berry, is that you?"

She turned around to see Jake Johnson coming towards her. "Uncle Jake" was actually the uncle of her cousin Maggie's husband, Marcus. Jake and his wife Molly were very close to Marcus and Maggie and together at nearly every family function. With no children of their own, Jake and Molly had "adopted" Sara's three children as extended family. Jake was a fixture at Jerry's Top Town Diner. She supposed that since he had sold his business to Marcus a few years ago, he spent more time here now than ever.

He gave her a big hug. She didn't know many "old school" manufacturers, but he was one of them, a big bear kind of a man with a larger-than-life personality and a classic pulled-himself-up-by-his-bootstraps story. He had started out working for someone else after a stint in the Marine Corps, and soon after, he'd launched his own business in the old pole barn behind his house. By the time he'd retired, he'd built a small machine shop that was perfectly suited for Marcus to launch his new business, Shelfwerx.

"I just got here," he said. "Do you want to join me? I have a table in the back."

"Why not?" she answered. "That would be great."

Jake was always interested in what she was working on, so after they caught up on the family, Sara shot him back a question. "Jake, how did you know it was time to sell?"

He looked at Sara for a moment and then said, "I don't think I ever *knew* it was time to sell. I ended up knowing that I *had* to sell after we beat Molly's cancer. Marcus using the machine shop to start Shelfwerx worked out for me in a way that I couldn't have planned for. I found out later that it could have taken me another three to five years to sell if I had gone the traditional route. What's going on, Sara?"

She told him about the letter and that she was seriously considering selling for the first time. Whether it was because Jake was just a good listener or because Sara knew he had been through a lot with Molly's cancer, all of her thoughts about the business came pouring out: she wasn't as excited about the company as she once had been. BerryBaby probably needed to grow again. Sara was tired and wasn't sure if she knew what was next.

Jake listened patiently and then said, "After everything, this is what I know. Things worked out for us but…. Well, you know me – I'm stubborn. I probably waited too long to think about it. Until Molly got sick, I just assumed that I would work until I couldn't because I liked everything about my business. I liked having my name on the door, being the boss, taking the risks – the whole enchilada. But looking back, as much as I liked it, I really put everything at risk because I hadn't thought much about how to sell my business. If I had done that, I could have probably kept the business *and* have the life Molly and I have now. Doing everything myself has probably been my biggest accomplishment and also one of my biggest mistakes."

"So what are you saying, Jake? Don't sell my business?" Sara asked.

"No," he answered carefully. "What I'm saying is I wish I had gotten my business ready to sell a lot sooner than I did so I would have had more choices. Maybe everything would have turned out the same. But I know now that while it felt great to help Marcus get Shelfwerx off the ground, in the end, I really didn't have many options in terms of selling my business when I did. And that's not something I'm very proud of."

Her cousin Maggie had told Sara that Molly and Jake had been frugal and had saved quite a bit, so they weren't hurting financially. But Sara could see how going from 40+ years of owning and running your own company to being essentially, if gainfully, unemployed could be a tough transition if you weren't prepared. Molly's cancer *had* changed everything. After Molly was in remission, Jake had quickly sold his business to Marcus, and he and Molly left for one of those "someday" trips they had been putting off.

Sara and Jake finished their lunch while catching up on other things. As they were leaving, Jake grabbed Sara's arm and said, "It sounds like this possible offer could be *exactly* what you're looking for, Sara. But I know someone who might be able to give you some insight on how to look at all of this from a different point of view. I think I have his contact information."

Jake reached into his wallet and gave Sara a card.

"Give him a call Sara," Jake said as they walked out the door. "I think he can help you."

- Are you as interested in your business now as you were five years ago?
- Do you have an advisor or a trusted resource to review your ideas with you?
- Have you considered what your exit strategy is for your business or your job?

CHAPTER 2

As she walked back to the office Sara thought about her conversation with Jake. She realized that waiting another 20 years to prepare for the future, as Jake had done, probably wasn't a good option for her or BabyBerry. She knew she should have worked on having a long-term plan for the company but somehow, over the years, she'd pushed those thoughts aside.

In the beginning, she and Kit were just trying to stay on top of the orders and her three small children. While she had fond memories of some of those early days of BabyBerry in her home, Sara was relieved when they had moved the company into town. Slowly, the business grew – just as her children had grown – from infants to toddlers to the awkward middle school years and now young adults. BabyBerry was ready for its next phase, but she wasn't quite sure what that looked like.

Running into Jake had extended her lunch; Sara slipped back into the office just before her meeting with Lydia. She dropped her coat in her office and walked down to Lydia's office. In the beginning, Kit and Sara had shared responsibility for almost everything at the company. Her mother had insisted that she didn't want an ownership stake and had asked to be an employee. "There can only be one boss, Sara," she'd told her daughter. Kit was more creative and liked the design side, while Sara enjoyed marketing, operations, and building the relationships they needed to be successful. They had shared ideas and had respected each other's opinions. While it probably wouldn't have worked for everyone, they had always figured it out.

It was Kit who'd pushed for Lydia's position as the Director of Design and Product Development. Sara had been concerned that there might be some friction with bringing someone new on board. But that friction never materialized. Maybe it was the age difference between Kit and Lydia, or the fact that Kit really did want to find the right replacement for herself at the company. Sara would sometimes find them so engrossed in working through the product development process that she knew not to disturb them. Slowly, wanting to give Lydia the room to create her own stamp at BabyBerry, Kit had reduced her role at the company. Over the last few years, Kit had seemed to know just the right time to stop by. Lydia would say to Sara, "Kit has the magic."

Lydia Winchester had been with BabyBerry for almost eight years. She had been the *perfect* person to fill that role. Her resume had come across Sara's desk when Lydia and her husband moved to town from Los Angeles. He had come to work for one of the new tech start-up companies. Lydia was amazed and thrilled that there was an opportunity to use her talents at BabyBerry. She had managed a small product development team for a boutique children's clothing line and had an amazing eye. In addition to understanding what BabyBerry needed to do to grow, expand, and develop the business, Lydia also had some great contacts in the industry. She had introduced Sara to the owner of her former company, who'd helped introduce Sara to some of his customers.

Sara knew that Lydia had become frustrated over the last year. Lydia had brought up a number of new ideas – some really good ones – but Sara found it hard to commit to anything new. She suspected that Lydia was becoming more than just a little annoyed by Sara's indecisiveness.

"Lydia has been a great *technical* replacement for Kit," Sara thought. But what she'd realized over the last few months was that Kit had also been Sara's perfect *advisor*. Lydia had taken over design and product development beautifully, but that only underscored how important Kit's role as a confidant and a second pair of eyes had really been to Sara. Talking to Jake today had reinforced that hunch.

Lydia and Sara ran through their standard agenda. After they were done, Lydia pushed back her chair. "Sara, normally I like to have my ideas solidified before I run them by you, but that email from Kelsey St. James got me thinking. Do you have a few more minutes?"

After Sara nodded her agreement, Lydia pulled out some old documents from her folder. "I went back into the archives and pulled out some old photos and sketches from the first years of BabyBerry."

She laid them out on the table in front of Sara. "Do you notice anything?"

Sara looked through them and smiled. The photography was barely professional, but there was no doubt that these were BabyBerry's original bags. While it was interesting to look at these old styles, she wasn't sure what Lydia wanted her to see. Sara looked up at Lydia. "I remember this photo shoot. It was probably our second or third year in business. I have a feeling I'm not seeing what you see though. What am I missing?"

"These designs are phenomenal!" Lydia exclaimed. "As soon as I saw the photo of Kelsey's mom holding that early BabyBerry bag, it gave me an idea. I'd like to put together our next collection based on these bags. I think the styles would be really well received. And...." Lydia stopped and drew a breath, "I'd like to do it to honor Kit. She meant a lot to me – to everyone."

Sara was quiet for a few moments. She looked at the photos again and said, "Well, everything comes back in style, right? I think it's a great idea if we can pull it off. Let's see the sketches, and we'll go from there."

Sara spent the rest of the day going through the monthly financials her CPA had sent over last week. While the numbers weren't terrible, sales had slipped slightly this past year and that was impacting the bottom line. They had gotten a boost a few years ago when they had updated the online store, but hadn't done much new since then.

She picked up the business card Jake had given her.

Bill McEntire, Tandem Wheels Partners – It Takes Two!

She thought about it a moment. Talking to Jake today about BabyBerry had felt like a relief. *Maybe this Bill McEntire could help her plot her next move?* Before she could change her mind, she crafted a quick email to him and left the office. Maybe Lydia's idea will slow our slide, she thought. It was a good thought to have as she drove home.

The next day Sara had an early morning breakfast meeting at the hospital. She was on the advisory board for the Pediatric and Infant Care Center there. Not uncommon with twins, Matt and Trevor were born two months early. Thankfully, neither had any serious health issues and both were able to come home slightly before their original due date. While having premature babies was challenging, Sara and Tom were always thankful for the care and kindness they and their family received. The hospital monitored "NICU" babies, and over the years Sara and Tom had supported its various fundraising events. Additionally, BabyBerry had been able to keep the hospital nursery's emergency pantry well-stocked for parents who were unprepared or unable to purchase the necessary supplies to take their newborn home.

Sara had felt particularly grateful she had been able to participate on the board over the past 10 years. It was a likeminded but diverse group of volunteers, and she felt their contributions had made a difference. With the town's growth over the past few years, the new Family Center was now reaching near capacity sooner than the hospital had anticipated. Affiliated with the hospital's birthing center, the Family Center served as an educational and support system to families of all socio-economic statuses. It had been cutting edge since its inception, and Sara had been proud to help steward it into the community. The original plans had included an expansion in five years, but as today's agenda suggested, it was now time to consider a new fundraising campaign.

Dr. Marti Phillips, the hospital's CEO, ran through the current and future projections along with their proposal. After her presentation was complete, she thanked the group. "It's due to many of you in this room that we owe our success, and with your continued support, we will provide the best possible care, support, and education to our families. I know it seems like yesterday that we were having a very similar conversation about Phase I of our expansion, but I'm excited to get started on Phase II and hope you are as well."

As Sara listened to Dr. Phillips, she remembered how unprepared she and Tom were those first few months and was thankful that the hospital now provided so many more services to young families. Once again, Sara was asked to be on the fundraising committee. For a moment, she thought about declining. I really should spend more time on BabyBerry, she thought, thinking about the financials she reviewed the day before. But this was something she felt strongly about. She would figure out a way to make everything work.

She arrived at the office and found an email response from Bill McEntire.

Sara,

Thank you for reaching out to me. I would love to learn more about BabyBerry. My wife and daughter-in-law are big fans.

I'm not sure what your availability is. We are leaving town on a trip tomorrow, but I could swing by this afternoon if you are free.

If not, shoot me some dates next week and we'll make it work.

Best,
Bill McEntire
It Takes Two!

Sara looked at her calendar. There was nothing that couldn't be rescheduled, and something told her she needed to have this conversation with Bill sooner than later. She responded to his email, and Bill confirmed for 1:00 p.m.

Char knocked on the door. "There's a Brad Thompson on the phone for you? He said he was referred by Tom."

Sara laughed. Char was the friendliest assistant in the business but incredibly protective of Sara's time. "Thanks, Char. You can put him through. They're old friends from law school."

"Hello, Sara," Brad's deep voice greeted her as she picked up the phone. "It's been a long time!"

"Hi, Brad. It certainly has. I really appreciate you taking some time to talk with me about this offer letter," Sara said. "Tom said you were going to do some digging?"

"I did." Brad went on tell Sara that Pine River Group was an M&A group that helped private equity and other firms make acquisitions. Brad had looked at some deals they had closed over the past two years and concluded that their client was most likely a holding company called Goodrich.

"Why do you think that it's Goodrich?" Sara asked.

"Well, Goodrich has recently acquired a full or partial stake in several other similar companies in the children's space – Stroller Baby, GoCO and LittleTyme," Brad told her. "It looks like the executive team at Stroller Baby is also involved in Goodrich. Are you familiar with any of these companies?"

The companies that Brad mentioned were some of the higher-end players in their market segment – strollers, furniture and accessories. They were the BabyBerry of their respective industries.

Brad went on to describe possible next steps for Sara and concluded by saying, "Sara, if you think you might be ready to sell, I would recommend getting a company valuation. From there you can do a gut check on what your number is. I would at least do a quick assessment before you have any conversations with anyone. These guys typically start at a higher number, and then they whittle it down with their due diligence process. Of course, don't sign anything until you know what you want to do."

Sara laughed, "Brad, you do remember I'm married to an attorney? Thanks for your help with all of this. I know you and

Tom are friends, but drop me an invoice in the mail for your time, please."

"I'm calling this a consult, Sara. But this is the work we do here, and if you decide to move forward, let me know. We can have a more serious conversation about next steps," Brad said. "Keep me posted either way, okay?"

Am I ready to sell? Sara asked herself. She didn't know, but she had a feeling after her meeting with Bill this afternoon, she would know more.

- What interests do you have outside of your business?
- How much time do you spend on activities outside of your business?
- How often do you meet with your key employees one-on-one?

CHAPTER 3

The morning went quickly, but Sara's upcoming visit with Bill McEntire kept popping into her head. She knew he had helped her cousin Maggie's husband Marcus get his business on track last year, and now it was growing by leaps and bounds. But Marcus's situation was so different from hers. Her company was nearly 20 years old and while not large, had been profitable from day one. Except for some minor bumps and one major bump (exploring overseas sourcing), they had done just fine.

She knew a little about Bill from Maggie and Marcus. Marcus had said, "Bill's a little quirky, but he's spot on. He helped me over the hump when I was stuck. He understood exactly what I needed to do to grow the business without going crazy."

Maggie had told her that Shelfwerx was probably going to double in sales again next year after winning a new account at one of the large grocery chains. Shelfwerx and BabyBerry were really at a different point of the business journey. Sara wasn't quite sure what Bill McEntire could do to help her.

Around 1:00 p.m., Char came into her office. "Bill McEntire is here to see you."

The quizzical look on Char's face made Sara ask, "What's up, Char?"

"It's 35 degrees outside and I think he *rode a bicycle* here today!" Char exclaimed. "Some people have no common sense!"

Sara laughed and went out to meet him. As soon as she saw Bill, she understood Char's comment. Bill must have been near 70, but while small in stature, he had a purpose and vitality that suggested a much younger man. In one hand he was carrying a bicycle helmet, and in the other a small bike pack.

"Bill, welcome to BabyBerry." She shook his hand and walked with him to her office. "Where should we get started?"

"How about a tour," Bill suggested. "I've found that's a good way to break the ice. How about in the shipping department? I always like to work my way backwards."

Sara suppressed a smile and thought, that doesn't surprise me at all! She guided Bill back into the warehouse and started the tour in the shipping department. It had been a while since she had taken anyone new through the plant. Bill asked great questions that made her think and remember how much they had accomplished over the past 20 years.

As they were walking through the crafters' room where the sewing machines and leather working area were set up, Bill commented, "I read your website and know that your mother made the first bag. How did you come up with the canvas and leather designs? I'm not an expert on baby accessories, but that seems unique."

"My grandfather was a plumber, and he carried one of the old 'plumber's bags,'" Sara laughed. "My mother always liked the efficiency of them, so she used that as her inspiration. Turns out canvas and leather wore well and were, at the time, relatively inexpensive. We've expanded to other materials along the way, but we've always kept at least some small component of the original bag in every design since."

They toured the customer service center and stopped by Darren's desk. As they were leaving, Darren said, "Sara, I already received that release from Kelsey St. James and her mother. I emailed you the case study template for approval."

Sara told Bill about the email that they'd received earlier in the week, and Bill smiled. "That certainly says something about BabyBerry."

She introduced Bill to Lydia and asked her to give a brief overview of what she did. When Lydia finished, Bill said to both of them, "It's obvious that a lot of pride and workmanship goes into every bag. Fascinating!"

As they walked back to her office, Sara noticed a strong feeling of nostalgia creeping into her thoughts. Bill must have read her mind, because he said, "It's amazing what a lifetime's work can do, isn't it?"

"Yes," she answered slowly, "it's been awhile since I've thought about all the twists and turns, let alone talked to someone about it."

As they sat down in Sara's office, she looked at Bill. "Now what? I'm not exactly sure why Jake thought you could help me or even how to figure that out."

Bill took out a small notebook from his bike pack. "Well, for starters, what prompted Jake to refer me to you?"

Sara sighed and pulled out the letter. "It all started with this. I've received inquiries to sell from time to time. Usually form letters from brokers – nothing serious. I didn't pay any attention to them or threw them in the trash. But, now – now it seems like it's something I might want to do. And in doing that, I feel more confused than ever."

"I understand," Bill said. "I've sold five businesses of my own and helped a number of people through the transition. I've found that even when the owner is 100% committed and looking forward to the sale, there can be a host of things that create issues."

"You've sold five businesses! Wow," Sara murmured. "How did you know when to sell?"

"Well, with each one it was a little different," he answered. "I had never planned on going into business at all. My parents had a small manufacturing company in Smithville, where I grew up. They made mailboxes."

Sara looked surprised, and Bill laughed. "All kinds of mailboxes – residential, commercial, apartment. It was a nice little business because everyone needs one! But I really wanted to be an engineer – build big things – not little mailboxes! It drove my father nuts. Well, I started working as an engineer and realized that while I liked the *idea* of designing things, I really enjoyed troubleshooting and problem-solving just as much. In my first job, engineers were kept out of the actual running of things, and I felt too isolated. My parents had run into some legal issues with patents. I became fascinated with the whole process and the attorney they hired to help them out. Before you know it, I was applying to law school."

"My husband is an attorney," Sara laughed. "My father says there are too many in the world already."

"I might have to agree with your father," Bill smiled. "Well, my dad became ill after my second year of law school, and I came home to help him out until he was back on his feet. I spent a year in the company and then went back to finish school. But by then, I was hooked. I was able to do some engineering design and business, and I liked everything about troubleshooting at the company."

"I'm surprised you hadn't discovered that before you left for college," Sara mused.

"My parents were second-generation Americans," he explained. "It was really important to them that their children went to college. I don't think they valued our little company as much as they could have. It employed almost 50 people in the peak years and put food on our table as well as on those of the families who worked there. And I might have had just a little stubbornness in me as well on wanting to strike out on my own."

Bill had a twinkle in his eye. "So my dad got better and I went back to law school. But right after graduation, my dad had a relapse and passed away about six months later. My parents hadn't done any planning for that scenario. Then a bigger competitor came in and offered my mother a deal that she didn't think she could refuse, so she sold the company."

Bill stopped for a moment, "I couldn't convince her differently. I think she didn't trust that my sister and I knew enough. She was so overwhelmed and worried about her life after my dad. She didn't want to be a burden."

Bill was quiet. Sara remembered how she felt about her company after Kit's passing and she could understand. Bill intuitively followed her train of thought. "I understand you recently lost your own mother, Sara. It's challenging to lose a parent – especially when you work side-by-side like that."

"Thank you, I'm sure you do understand. So, what did you do next?"

"Well, during the year I had worked for my parents, I had come up with a couple of patents for some new types of commercial mailboxes. My dad made sure that I registered them personally instead of doing it through the business. I think even then he knew something might happen to him. I'll be forever grateful for that move. Remember that attorney I told you about, the one that got me interested in law?"

She nodded.

"Well, he saw something in these ideas and helped me start my own company. And I ran that for the next 25 years until my son took it over," Bill said. "Of course, I also bought a construction company that I had no business buying. But after a few years, we figured out a way to turn a profit. I sold that about five years later."

Bill looked at Sara and asked, "Sara, so what is your dilemma here? It sounds like you have a nice business, and you may have a suitable offer on the table. Obviously, we don't know yet, but it looks somewhat promising. It sounds like it *could* be perfect timing."

"You sound like my husband," she answered him carefully. "But it doesn't *feel* like perfect timing."

"What would make it perfect?" Bill asked.

"I'm not sure," Sara laughed ruefully. "Something is nagging at me that I'm missing something, but I don't know what it is. I asked you earlier about knowing when to sell, and you said that each one was different. What did you mean by that?"

"Well, with my parent's business, my mother didn't trust me or my sister to run the business – or herself, for that matter, so that decision, I would say, was based on fear. Fear of failing or being a burden to her family if the business failed. I wouldn't recommend that one because I think it left some regret on the table," Bill said. "After that experience, I realized the importance of thinking about what's next. And sometimes 'what's next' isn't the founder running the business. I mentioned the construction company?"

Sara nodded.

"The company I started after my parents' business was sold did very well," he smiled. "I was certain that I had the Midas touch and could do anything. One of our customers was a construction company that specialized in interior finishes for apartment buildings, and they got into some trouble. I agreed to purchase a significant share of the company to help them out. Of course, I had been selling to them for years so I thought I *knew* them and the industry. We lost almost everything."

"Wow." Sara thought about losing BabyBerry and shuddered. "But you said you turned it around?"

"We did, finally," Bill answered. "And it was painful. In order to get out of the mess, we had to shrink to survive. We had to lay off long-term employees at *both* companies to keep things running. It was not something I was proud of."

"I bet that was hard," Sara said, thinking of Carol Ann and Consuela and the rest of her team.

"It was. And it should have been hard. I was pretty full of myself in those days. In almost losing everything, I learned a few things," he smiled. "And I don't think I would be here talking to you if it hadn't happened that way."

"That is probably true," Sara said. "Bill, if you were me, what would you do?"

"Sara, I think that's something you'll have to decide on your own." He paused. "But this is what I do know. There are only four ways an owner leaves his or her business – selling to a new owner, transitioning to children or employees, liquidating, or leaving with 'their boots on.' If you don't adequately prepare for the first two options, the second two are often your only choices. The real question is: which of those four options are you prepared for?"

Sara was quiet. BabyBerry was a good business. It had been profitable almost since the beginning and, along with her family, had occupied most of the past 20 years of her life. Her customers loved their products, and the company was starting to see the next generation of buyers. But somehow in the busyness, Sara hadn't really thought of what the future would hold for her or the company when it was time for her to step away.

She looked at Bill. "I'm not sure, Bill. But I think it's time to find out."

By the time Bill left that afternoon, it was near the end of the day. Sara caught up on some emails and checked in with her husband. Tom agreed with her that stopping for dinner sounded like a great idea; they would meet over at the Oak Tavern on the way home. Sara looked at her watch. She still had about an hour before meeting Tom.

For most of her working life, Sara had come in early and left by late afternoon to accommodate her children's activities. As the twins approached college, she found that the newfound flexibility in her schedule allowed her to stay later in the day. She realized that she was neither an early morning person nor a night owl, but she did enjoy the quieter environment at the end of the day after the majority of the BabyBerry employees had left.

Char had poked her head into Sara's office before she left. "Sara, I'm going to leave for the day. You and Lydia are the last ones here. Do you need anything?"

"Thanks, Char, I'm just going to finish up before I meet Tom for dinner. Have a good night," Sara answered. She pulled out her notes from Bill's visit. They had set up a meeting for next week after Bill returned from his trip. In the meantime, he had given her a small homework assignment, and she'd tackle that tomorrow.

Bill had asked a lot of questions that had made Sara reflect on the past 20 years. But one question stood out in her mind. *What would she do if she no longer owned BabyBerry?* She couldn't easily answer the question. Bill didn't push her, but his insights rang true.

"Sara, from my experience, most successful entrepreneurs or business owners all have some kind of vision as it relates to their businesses," Bill commented. "Interestingly, many do not have a vision for their "after business" life, and that's how they get into trouble."

"I'm not sure I understand," Sara said.

Bill thought for a moment. "When we *don't* have something to look forward to or work towards, it's much too easy to look backwards. And often, in spending too much time looking back, we tend to have regrets about how things 'should' have been different," he said. "I think it's human nature – if you're excited about the future, you're less concerned about what you did or didn't do in the past. It's only when we feel stuck or directionless that the past controls our thinking. I have seen this consistently play out regardless of how much an owner has received from the proceeds of a sale. By nature, business owners like having something to do, and even better if it's something with a purpose or that we have a passion for."

Sara understood what Bill was saying. Once she decided to turn BabyBerry into a business, she put her heart and soul into the company with few regrets. Not that it always was easy, but she rarely minded making the sacrifices the company required. Somewhat like parenting, she chuckled.

Lydia's knock on her door interrupted her thoughts. "I'm heading out, Sara."

"I'm on my way out too. I'll walk out with you." Sara gathered her things and walked out with Lydia.

"I spent most of the afternoon going through the archives, and I'm pretty excited about some of the things I've found," Lydia said. "I should have the sketches done by next week."

"I think you are onto something, Lydia," Sara told her. "I'm looking forward to seeing your ideas. I think it could be a great way to celebrate our 20th anniversary."

Lydia smiled. "Thanks. I think it will be a fun project for everyone."

They said good night in the parking lot, and Sara made her way to meet Tom for dinner. The Oak Tavern had been hosting weary travelers since the 1800s. Small and dark, the historic inn no longer provided lodging, but it was one of Tom and Sara's favorite places to have dinner and relax after a long day. With its cozy booths and thick stone walls, it was relatively quiet even during the busiest of dinner rushes.

Tom had arrived a few minutes ahead of Sara, and had secured a table as well as a glass of wine for her. After she settled in, he asked, "So how did it go with the infamous Bill McEntire? Is he as quirky as Maggie and Marcus described?"

Sara thought for a moment. "Well, yes and no. I really enjoyed talking to him. He really does know his stuff, and my head is spinning with everything we discussed. But, yes, he is a little quirky. You should have seen the look on Char's face when she realized he had ridden his bicycle to the office."

Tom laughed. "Poor Char. I'm guessing Bill didn't pass her common sense meter by riding a bicycle in the winter!"

Sara smiled, "Exactly!"

The server interrupted their conversation to take their order. After he left, Sara shared the highlights of her meeting with Bill. When she was done, Tom said, "It sounds like you covered a lot of territory today. Did you get the answers you were looking for?

Sara sighed. "I wanted to understand the selling process a bit more, and he was able to help with that. He's sold a couple of businesses himself as well as helped other people like me position their businesses for sale. He asked a lot of great questions. Unfortunately, a few stumped me."

"Such as?" Tom asked.

"Well, the big question was, 'What would I do after I sold BabyBerry?' And I have no idea. That always seemed like such a faraway goal," Sara laughed. "We've been saving for retirement and looking at the kids finishing college as the big milestones in our lives. It dawned on me the real hurdle is that we *both* have businesses that are going to have to be sold or transferred *if* we want or need to stop working. I think losing Mom this year may have started me down this path, but I realize now this would have probably come up in the next year or two as the kids move out on their own. In my mind, it's always been something for a tomorrow that's far away. Except, in reality, tomorrow has already become today."

They were both quiet for a few moments, and Sara could tell that Tom was thinking about his own situation, back when he was with a prestigious law firm practicing real estate and business law. He had enjoyed what he did and was good at it. But even though he was on a partner track, he had realized that there was something in him that wanted a practice that would allow him to blaze his own trail. So after five years, he'd started his own firm, one that focused on his areas of expertise. Tom had done well, and she knew he'd never regretted leaving the larger practice.

Sara looked at him and asked, "Remember when you first started at the firm and there were all those retired and semi-retired partners who still were coming into the office?"

Tom nodded and Sara went on, "I hadn't thought about them in years until Bill started asking me what I was going to do if I sold the company. I remember us laughing about how they just couldn't quit. Without a plan to do otherwise, we're not really that much different."

Tom smiled. "Well, that's when we were young and knew everything. Now we're older and not as wise!"

They both laughed. Sara became somber. "I realized today that BabyBerry is an important part of who I am and I'm not sure what that means for the future."

Their conversation drifted onto other things, and Tom filled her in on a meeting with a new client. As she followed Tom home after dinner, Sara knew that while she didn't have all the answers, today had been an important day in understanding how she would find them.

- Have you planned to have someone replace you in your business?
- Do you know what the value of your business is?
- Has your tomorrow become today?

CHAPTER 4

The week flew by. Bill had asked Sara to gather some information for their next meeting about BabyBerry that would be helpful in evaluating the company's readiness to sell. He had also sent her some articles on selling a business that he thought would be of interest to her while she sorted through her own unanswered questions. When she left the office on Friday, she felt prepared and was looking forward to her next meeting with him.

After a restful weekend, Sara arrived at the office early on Monday. Knowing she had a busy day, she wanted some time to review her notes before her regular meetings and her afternoon meeting with Bill. Reviewing the information again, she knew that sales had been flat. She realized that it had been a while since she'd reviewed her company information with a critical eye. She made a few additional notes on some ideas she wanted to review with Bill and went to meet her team for the Weekly.

When Bill arrived promptly after lunch, Sara felt prepared. As he sat down at the conference table in Sara's office and looked at the papers in front of her, he laughed. "It looks like you did your homework!"

Sara smiled. "You know, it was a good exercise to pull this information together. It helped me look at the business in a way I hadn't done in a while and sparked a few ideas that I'd like to talk to you about."

"Excellent," Bill said, pulling out a tablet from his pack. "We're going to take your information and put it into this database to see where BabyBerry stands."

They reviewed the data Sara had pulled together until they had gone through everything and Sara had answered all of his questions. Finally, he looked at her and asked, "So do you have any questions? Do you think we missed anything?"

Sara had tons of questions, but she was eager to see the results of their labors, so she deferred for now and they dug in. The information they had input generated a report showing the strengths and weaknesses in how a buyer would look at Sara's company.

Strengths:
- Profitable
- Excellent reputation
- Customer loyalty – both direct and retailers

- Opportunity for growth
- Steady cash flow

Weaknesses:
- Owner highly involved in the business
- Supplier diversity was low
- Declining margins
- High dependency on key employees
- Repeatable business.

While the strengths were obvious to Sara and didn't surprise her, she was somewhat disheartened and tried not to be defensive as Bill ran through the report. Bill, sensing Sara's frustration, suggested they take a break.

When they returned Bill asked, "Sara, I know this is a lot of information to take in. Tell me what's bothering you the most?"

Sara thought for a minute and then answered, "With the great customer feedback and being profitable all of these years, I felt like BabyBerry was successful. Now, according to this analysis, it seems exactly the opposite of what I've focused on with my accountant."

"It was and is – because it is valuable to you, your customers, and, I expect, your employees. Through that lens, the company is extremely valuable. BabyBerry provided your customers a product they needed or wanted. It gave meaningful work and a livelihood to you and your employees," Bill answered. "Let me ask you this – would someone pay $1,000 for one of your bags?"

Sara laughed, "No, I'm afraid not. We do enjoy a premium price, but not quite that high."

"Exactly," Bill smiled. "So, similarly, BabyBerry *as a company* is only worth what a prospective acquirer wants to pay for it."

Sara was quiet for a moment. As painful as it was to hear what Bill was saying, she suddenly saw her business differently. For years, it was a passion that she shared with Kit, and then with the employees who came afterwards.

"You know what's odd?" Sara asked thoughtfully. "Tom and I have been diligent about saving for our retirement and paying for the kids' college – making it almost automatic. But we realized the other night that neither of us had spent much time thinking about what that life would look like after our businesses. I think it's because we've both really enjoyed our work. The irony is that our businesses are probably worth more than what we've saved so far, and yet we probably pay more attention to the number on our investment statements than the number you just gave me."

Bill gave Sara a moment longer with her thoughts and then said, "Sara, that shift you just made is key. Some business owners never get there because they limit the discomfort they're willing to experience in going through this process. These are the same people who overcome the many difficult challenges in starting and building their businesses. Strangely enough, they are absolutely unwilling to do what is required to prepare for a transition or a sale."

"I think I know what you mean. In the beginning, I didn't always know what I was getting into, and I didn't feel like I had much to lose," Sara mused.

Bill laughed. "Yes, sometimes it's *not* seeing what awaits us on the other side of the mountain that keeps us from turning back. Interesting, isn't it? There is so much emphasis on starting and managing businesses, but less so on selling or transitioning."

"It's almost like having children," Sara said thinking of her work with the NICU at the hospital. "It is a lot easier for the hospital to raise money for the Family Center than a hospice facility. Though coming into this world, for most of us, is a lot easier than leaving."

"I like to think there are many phases of owning a business. Start-up or acquisition, building and managing, preparing to sell or transition, the actual sales or transition process, and then life afterwards," Bill said. "I don't think I fully learned that until I transitioned my last business to my children. Strangely enough, I think that's when I found my true passion."

"What do you mean?" Sara asked.

"Well, because I had gone through the process before, and as I told you, almost lost everything when I bought the construction company, I knew the importance of having a business that was always ready to sell – even if I wasn't planning on selling in the short term. But this time, I wasn't planning on purchasing another company, so I had to think about what I wanted my life to be afterwards. That's how I came to do what I do now. I can honestly say the work I've done over the last 10 years has been more rewarding than I could have ever imagined."

"Is that how you developed the *Tandem Leadership* system?" Sara asked.

Bill smiled. "You must have been speaking with Marcus! What do you know about *Tandem Leadership?*"

Sara laughed. "Not much, really. Marcus had said it was helpful when he was feeling overwhelmed and Shelfwerx started taking off. But I did know enough *not* to be surprised when you showed up riding a bike!"

Bill laughed. "Your assistant is not the first person to think it odd!"

"So, tell me," Sara ventured, "how does the *Tandem Leadership* model help someone like me? Shelfwerx and BabyBerry are really at different stages. Marcus has only a few years into Shelfwerx and, well, BabyBerry is almost as old as my children!"

Bill sat back in his chair. "Riding a bicycle, from the time I was very young, always felt like freedom to me. It's the foundation of the *Tandem Leadership* model. Simply stated, it's how the business leader and her #2 work together. Have you ever tried to ride a unicycle?"

Sara shook her head.

"Well, riding a unicycle takes some practice. But once you know how, it can be pretty entertaining. I like using this example because most entrepreneurs all remember what it was like to wear many hats and juggle multiple priorities. Most of us get pretty good at it, and so sometimes we don't want to give up that skill as we need to add people to our team." Bill looked at Sara. "I suspect your experience might be a little different because you and your mother started the company together. By all accounts, it was a partnership that worked well."

Sara nodded. "We were fortunate that we got along so well. But I do understand what you mean. Between the business and my three children, we both had our hands full!"

"I suspect you did," Bill chuckled. "But if you compare the unicycle and the bicycle, the unicycle says 'look at me' while the bicycle says 'join me.' The bicycle needs two wheels – regardless of the number of seats on it. But each wheel has its own purpose. The back wheel is rigid, provides stability, and creates momentum. The front wheel can turn as it needs, and take the bike in any direction. I suspect that you and your mother worked together much like a bicycle from the start."

"I think there may have been times when it *felt* like a unicycle," Sara said thoughtfully.

Bill went on, "The *Tandem Leadership* process takes into account the joint but separate roles that a CEO and her #2 use to run the business. For a new CEO, it's the way I get her to understand that she can no longer ride around on her unicycle. If she wants to grow her company and grow her people, most CEOs need at least one #2 to be really successful."

Sara was perplexed. "That makes sense for someone starting their business, like Marcus and Shelfwerx. But I'm not really sure how it applies to BabyBerry or me."

"For a seasoned CEO or owner who is looking for an exit, or perhaps just not wanting to work so much, the roles on the bicycle can be changed so eventually a new leader can emerge and the organization can move forward without being as dependent on the owner," Bill answered. "I like to think of it as the difference between being a bicycle rider and a bicycle builder."

Sara thought of the conversations she had had with Marcus about the positive impact Bill had on him and his company. Even in the short time she had known him, she suspected Bill had impacted many other companies in the same way, and this was his not-so-subtle way of letting her know that she could think of a future beyond BabyBerry should she choose a different path.

"I've already proven that I can start and build a company – now maybe it's time for the next challenge," Sara ventured.

They spent the remainder of the afternoon reviewing the report and brainstorming future opportunities. Soon they had generated a list showing Sara there were some avenues for growth and increasing the company's profitability that she hadn't considered before. She was surprised to notice herself becoming more engaged and thinking more positively about the future. She couldn't believe that it was almost five o'clock when Bill turned his tablet off and pushed back from her conference table.

He looked at her and asked, "How do you feel?"

Sara smiled, "To be honest, at first it felt like I had been hit by a truck. But I think that was by design to grab my attention. Now, I can feel a little spark and am thinking about what else I could be doing with the company. But if your numbers are correct, BabyBerry isn't worth what I think it should be, and that concerns me. I'm not sure what next steps are."

"Well, let's talk about that for a minute," Bill answered. "What do you think your options are?"

Sara took a moment to consider Bill's question. "I could reach out to Pine River and see what they have to offer, but knowing that I could be leaving money on the table, that makes me uncomfortable. And, as you pointed out, I'm not really sure what I would do if I *weren't* running BabyBerry, and that's a problem too. Obviously, I could keep going as I have been but…well, I can't 'unlearn' what you've shared with me today, and that means something has to change."

"Sara, let me ask you this. Let's just say *you did know* what you should do and you could do anything you wanted. What do you think your plan would be?" Bill asked.

Sara went quiet. She hadn't been entirely truthful with herself or Bill. The "little spark" that she had mentioned seemed to be getting stronger. It was a familiar feeling, and it reminded her of those early years when she had started the business and she was excited to tackle the challenges that were in front of her. Suddenly she knew.

"I would want to run BabyBerry with the passion that I had at the beginning of my business." Sara looked at Bill. "I think of the story of your mother selling the company because she thought *she had to*. I don't want that to be one of my choices. Ultimately, I would want the freedom to know that I could sell if I wanted to, but that I didn't have to. And, lastly, I thought about my own mother today every time we came up with a new idea to expand or improve the business. Remember when I told you that Lydia is working on a new collection to honor some of our earliest designs?"

Bill nodded and Sara went on, "She wants to do it to honor Kit's legacy at BabyBerry. She was a part of everything we did here. But now thinking about it, having BabyBerry last beyond both of us seems like the ultimate way of honoring and preserving her legacy. I guess if I could have anything, that's what I would want."

Bill smiled. "Why can't you have those things, Sara?"

Sara couldn't think of one reason. And later, as she relayed the events of her afternoon to Tom that evening at home, Sara found she was even more excited than she had been that afternoon.

Tom noticed as well. "Sara, this is quite a turnaround for a week's work."

"I know. It sure feels that way to me too," Sara reflected. "It was almost as if …"

Tom finished her sentence, "… Kit was there too?"

Sara nodded.

Tom smiled. "Who says she wasn't?"

- Can you easily list the strength and weaknesses of your business?
- How often do you review opportunities to improve?
- Can you name the key elements that would attract a buyer to your business?

CHAPTER 5

Tom was thrilled to hear about Sara's meeting with Bill, but suggested she follow up with Brad Thompson. Sara agreed. "Bill said when the time comes to sell, it would be a good idea to have a team of advisors on our side," she said. "Knowing Brad's background, I'd love to have his opinion as well. I'll give him a call and set something up for us to meet with him. I'd like for both of us to understand what our options are when we're ready to sell."

The information that Bill had uncovered in their last meeting became the foundation of the plan they had agreed to work on together. While Bill's analysis showed a number of areas that needed attention, they had prioritized the top three items:

- Identifying opportunities for sales growth
- Reducing owner involvement in the day-to-day running of the company
- Balancing supplier and employee dependency to mitigate risk

"I've found that at this stage, it's better to start with the top three," Bill had said. "We'll review periodically and adjust course as needed. Plus, it's nearly impossible to focus on more than three things at once!"

Based on the brainstorming they had done under each of these categories, Sara had a set of action items, and she agreed to carve one hour each day to tackle her list. Bill had also asked her to start working on her new "map."

"Many CEOs and entrepreneurs are by nature, very vision-focused," he'd explained. "But they sometimes have blinders on when it comes to life after they sell. If they're serial entrepreneurs, they'll most likely just buy or start another business. But for some, and I suspect this may be you, so much of their lives are wrapped in their business that the "what's next" doesn't occur to them until after they no longer have a business. Using those visionary skills early in the process to create a new map and practicing their new life in advance can make the transition much easier."

"I think I understand," Sara had said, recalling her conversation with Jake a few weeks earlier. "I think that's what Jake was trying to tell me when he said he was happy that Marcus had bought Shelfwerx, but that he really wasn't as prepared for the future as he'd thought."

Bill's MAP process – Mindfully Aware and Prepared – asked a set of questions that Sara was to work through every day for the next week. It included questions on the activities and interests that she had enjoyed as a child as well as those she was participating in now. She was surprised how much she enjoyed this short process every day, and also surprised by the results. At the end of the week, Bill had asked her to send him the entire list with her top five experiences or activities highlighted. He also asked her to answer this question: "Without my business, I would…."As she reviewed her list, she found herself a little sad about the activities she had let go. This was Sara's list:

1. House Renovation – We bought our old farmhouse and restored it. Everyone said it would be a nightmare of a project, but I was a little sad when it was completed. Tom and I have talked about buying another house so we could do this again but haven't so far.

2. Hospital Advisory Board – It fits into BabyBerry's mission, and it's also very personal because of having had premature babies. I've been saying that when I have more time I would increase my participation on the board, but I haven't.

3. Physical Health – I was very active growing up, but have become less so than I'd like to be.

4. Travel – I'd always hoped Tom and I would pick a new destination to explore each year, but somehow that hasn't happened.

5. Mentor – I've been asked a few times by the University Business College to speak to their business students. I'd

like to think about working with new entrepreneurs and helping them with their businesses.

Lydia had let Sara know that she had completed her initial plans for the next season's lines, so on Friday morning they met to review them. As Lydia was talking, it was obvious to Sara that this project had been a labor of love for her. No detail was left undone – not only were the designs on trend, but so was the story behind each original bag's genesis. In the beginning, Sara hadn't really understood what Lydia had in mind when she proposed this project. But now she realized that it truly did honor her mother, and really, the entire BabyBerry experience.

After Lydia was done with her presentation, Sara was quiet for moment, processing, and then smiled. "This is amazing, Lydia! I love how it tells the story and also makes each design feel fresh and contemporary."

Lydia beamed and said, "Thank you, Sara. I have never felt so inspired before. Hopefully, the customers will feel the same way. I'd like to get this over to the agency so they can start working on supporting creative for the website and collateral. Would you like me to set up a meeting for us to review with them?"

"I think that's a great idea, but why don't you go ahead and have the initial meeting without me," Sara said. Noticing the surprised look on Lydia's face, she went on, "This was your idea, and you've carried it through beautifully."

"Thanks, Sara," Lydia said. "That means a lot to me."

"Kit trusted you, and so do I. I'm excited to see what you'll both come up with." Sara said, and meant it.

Tom had agreed to pick up Sara for their lunch meeting with Brad Thompson. When they arrived at the restaurant, the host ushered them back to a table where Brad was seated. After their initial pleasantries, Brad said, "I know Tom has a meeting this afternoon, so why don't we look at the menu first and then we can get caught up?"

After they'd ordered, Brad asked, "Sara, so where would you like to start?"

Sara reviewed the events over the past few weeks and shared with him what she had learned from Bill.

"Bill McEntire?" Brad laughed. "I've worked with Bill on a couple of deals where he's helped the company get ready for sale. The clients he works with always seem to be more prepared than some of my other clients!"

"Well, that's good to hear," Sara said. "Based on Bill's 'back of the napkin' evaluation, as he likes to call it, it seems like we would be leaving money on the table. After spending so much time on BabyBerry for the past 20 years, that doesn't sit well with me. With Bill's help, I think we can shore it up and see a better return."

"Sara," Brad said, "I'm sure Bill already told you this, but one of the biggest regrets I hear from owners who sell their business is that they think they could have done a better job in preparing for the sale, and that ultimately, they didn't get the proceeds they think they deserved. It's the nature of the sales process for the acquirers to negotiate for the lowest price, and for many sellers that feels like a slap in the face. Even the most savvy business owners I know struggle with having someone calling their 'baby' ugly!"

Sara laughed at Brad's unintentional pun. "I can see that now. When Bill was reviewing the results, I felt like I had been shocked awake. The way that we have looked at the business all these years and compared to the way our CPA firm looks at our business – the metrics are very different. However, I feel like my eyes are open now. But I do have a few questions for you."

Sara went on to tell Brad about the changes that she wanted to make at BabyBerry, including increasing sales, making the business run more effectively, and reducing the amount of time she spent on day-to-day activities. She asked what he'd recommend as next steps.

"First, I've known Bill for about 15 years, and I have a great deal of respect for him. It sounds like he's nailed down some great first steps for you to consider if you want to get the maximum value," Brad answered. "But there are at least two things that I think, intentionally or unintentionally, cause deals to fall through or owners to get cold feet. One is that the owner doesn't have a clear vision of what their future is going to be like after the sale. Either they find some reason to cancel the deal or are miserably unhappy afterwards. Second, they don't choose the right acquirer for their business."

"What do you mean, the 'right acquirer'?" Tom asked.

"Well, for example, in BabyBerry's case, you have a great brand and great products," Brad said. "Someone could buy BabyBerry to add to a portfolio of companies, which is what I'm assuming that Pine River and Goodrich are thinking. Bundled together with the other companies, they could create purchasing and sales synergies between the brands to get better deals and create leverage with distributors. They could also combine everything under one brand, or even a completely new brand, and then sell the whole thing as a vertically integrated package to another acquirer. They could also choose to just buy the brand name and introduce new products to fit another strategy that supports their overall portfolio."

"Which could mean that BabyBerry as an entity could cease to exist," Sara murmured. "I know this happens all the time, but I never thought about it in terms of my own company."

Sara thought about her meeting with Lydia that morning, and how they had talked about the importance of the BabyBerry legacy. She looked at Brad. "I'm sure there are other buyer motives I should consider?"

"Well, in your case, it wouldn't be unheard of for a buyer who just looks for brand names and then either outsources the products or combines them with other brands they own. While this isn't always a top priority for a seller, I think for owners who want to protect their employees, this can be a big shock," Brad answered. "Knowing *why* someone wants to purchase your company can be a deal breaker in some of the transactions I've worked on. And, for others it doesn't matter at all."

Sara thought for a moment and looked at Tom and then Brad. "When Tom and I 'rescued' our old farm house, everyone thought we should just tear it down and start over. I felt like it was our responsibility to restore it and bring it back to life. But we could just as easily have torn it down."

"Exactly," Brad answered. "Because our businesses usually include people – our customers, our supplier, and our employees – it's important to many of our clients that those relationships remain intact, if they can. Knowing what's important to you in the sale can go miles toward avoiding seller's regret."

By the end of lunch, Brad had reviewed a number of other suggestions and ideas for Sara and Tom to consider. She had told Brad about *Tandem Leadership* and Bill's philosophy of having a strong #2 in the lead role as they were closer to exit.

"I think that's wise, Sara, and this is why. Even with the strongest financials and the most nailed-down business plans, buyers like to have the sellers have some stake in the outcomes. For companies with high owner involvement in the day-to-day, it can mean having to stay on another two years after the close. I rarely see anyone last much past a year and this usually means leaving some money on the table. If you can work that out before the sale, it may be worth it to you."

Before they left, Sara asked Brad if he would consider being on their "advisor team" and putting together a proposal for ongoing support. Brad agreed and said, "Sara, it's been fun watching you build BabyBerry over the years, but I have a feeling the best is yet to come."

Sara hoped that Brad was right.

- Without my business I would…?
- Who would you include on your team of advisors to sell your business?
- Have you reviewed your long-term plans for the business with your CPA?

CHAPTER 6

The next week Bill asked Sara to come to his office in Smithville for their meeting. She had jotted down the address without much thought and smiled when her car's navigation system announced her arrival. It was the company that Bill had started after law school and that company was now owned by his son and daughter. His son had become president while his daughter, an attorney, was not active in the day-to-day running of the business. Bill had told Sara that he and his wife still owned the building and that he kept a small office there.

"As any good owner in a sale, I agreed to help out," Bill told her after he escorted her back to his office. "But my wife would never forgive me if our son had any issues running the business. Thankfully, he inherited my good looks and his mother's brains!"

Sara laughed. Bill's sense of humor was starting to grow on her. She thought about how Kit had stayed on after Lydia had come to BabyBerry. Kit had known how to support Lydia without getting in her way. She was coming to realize what a gift that had been to both of them. Apparently transitions didn't always happen so easily.

After they both donned safety glasses, Bill toured Sara through the plant. It was with obvious pride that Bill showed the numerous improvements that the company had made since his son Will had taken over the company. Bill knew everyone by name, and there was mutual affection between Bill and everyone they spoke with.

"Automated machining has changed so much of the dynamics of this place," Bill said. "Will has been much more future-focused than I ever was at his age. The efficiencies they have been able to deploy have really made a difference in the quality and the flexibility of what they can produce."

Sara noticed an electronics area and asked Bill what they were doing, "It's a new project that they've taken on," he told her. "Electronic locks for a corporate mailroom that processes payments. My father would be so surprised to see what his grandson is up to these days."

At the end of the tour, Bill introduced Sara to his son, and Sara suppressed a smile. Will really was a clone of Bill – just thirty years younger. He greeted Sara warmly and teased his father, "Don't listen to everything the old man says, Sara. Our Celtic family origins lend to tall tales."

"We'll see you tonight at the dance recital," Bill said and shook his head. "Will has two daughters, and I cannot tell you the number of dance recitals his mother and I have been to!"

They settled into Bill's office. While Bill went to grab them some coffee, Sara looked around. There were many photos of Bill and his family, including some of a young Bill with who Sara imagined were his parents and his sister in front of his family's first business, McEntire Metal Co. She noticed several awards from local charities and some trophies from bicycle races in the senior age division.

When Bill returned to the room, Sara looked up. "I see you're quite the racer!"

"You know what's interesting about that," Bill said as they took their seat around the conference table. "I think I told you that riding my bicycle had always meant freedom to me. But until I sold this company to Will, I hadn't really ridden a bike since I was in high school. It was part of my 'business owner recovery therapy' as I was transitioning to my new life."

That admission floored Sara. The way that Bill had spoken about transitioning a business, she assumed that he had always been clear-headed and focused about the process. Sara must have looked puzzled because Bill seemed to read her mind. "As I said, I learned something new each time I participated in a sale," he said. "The lesson I didn't learn until this last one was to truly have a passion and a purpose outside of the business. I had always gone from one business adventure to the next. The challenge of moving to a new venture always smoothed the transition. Without having a new company to focus on, something had to change – and that something was me!"

"How did you rediscover cycling?" Sara asked.

"My oldest grandchild was learning to ride a bicycle, and she liked having her old Grandpa there to help her," Bill said. "One day I mentioned to my daughter that it brought me back to my own childhood. For my birthday, Will and Clare bought me a bicycle to ride with the grandkids, and I never looked back. Of course, it became a little bit of an obsession."

Bill pointed to some photos behind his desk. Sara noticed right away that the photos of Bill in his cycling clothes were of a different bicycle in each photo. He laughed, "You know, it's never the rider's fault you lose a race! I've been told that I'm no longer able to buy a new one until I trade in an old one. Some people like collecting cars...."

Bill pulled out Sara's email from the previous week. "So what does your list tell us, Sara?"

Sara had been anticipating this question since Bill had told her to make the list and answer the question of what she would do if she were no longer running BabyBerry. "I think it would be more than one thing," she said. "I thought about Jake and how he and Molly took their trip around the world. As I said, I wouldn't mind doing some exploring, but I'm not interested in doing it for months on end."

"I can understand that," Bill answered.

Sara went on, "Outside of my family and my business, I am probably most proud of being on the Family Center Advisory Board at the hospital and of what we've been able to accomplish. I think there will be more opportunities there as the new fundraising campaign starts."

"I'm sure they could use you as well," Bill said.

"I also really enjoyed renovating our old farmhouse as well as the old factory the BabyBerry offices are in. I loved pulling off those projects," Sara said, "Tom and I have discussed a number of times buying other houses to renovate, but I've never seemed to find the time. Until this exercise, I had forgotten that both of our contractors said that I had a knack for both the execution and the design. If I had the time, I think it's something I would really enjoy doing."

They spent the first hour of their meeting reviewing the rest of the items on Sara's list until she could see that there were actually many things she was interested in. What she and Bill laid before her was very different than her current life. It intrigued her, but she felt uncomfortable as well. The world in which she had the time and the energy to do all these things felt very far away.

"Do you know why we created this list?" Bill asked her.

"No, I'm afraid not," Sara answered.

"At our most basic level, we are motivated by two things – to avoid pain and seek pleasure." Bill answered. "If we think that moving out of our role as the owner will be painful, we'll avoid it."

Sara nodded and Bill went on, "But I've found that when enticing a business owner to look forward or beyond her current business situation, she needs a carrot, something that is much more interesting to her than her current position or even her company. I believe that's why there are so many serial entrepreneurs. We simply replace one venture for the next without even realizing it. However, for some of us, there comes a time when a business – any business – no longer holds our interest. And we need the passion from our business to support the purpose of our lives."

"So what you are saying is that I need to be thinking about my life after BabyBerry *before* I sell the company?" Sara asked.

"Yes, and here's why," Bill answered. "If you don't have a forward focus or something you really want to do with your life afterwards, it can create problems. One is to sabotage the transition with your leadership team. Sometimes I see owners drag their feet in the tasks around the sale itself. Most of the time it's unconscious, but it still creates problems for everyone involved. Building the life that you want after the sale, in advance, is the easiest way to avoid those roadblocks. It's what I call the 'bike builder' phase. You're guiding your team to ride the bike without you, which creates a new framework for the business."

"I think that makes sense," Sara said, "but I'm not exactly sure how this is going to work if I'm putting extra time into growing my sales and improving my business."

"Let's talk about that," Bill responded. "If you were out of commission for a month, what do you think would happen at work?"

Sara thought for a moment. "Lydia, Darren, and Carol Ann would all step up and keep things running."

Bill smiled, "How long do you think that could go on – without you?"

"Probably a few months," Sara admitted. "Darren and Carol Ann would handle the majority of the day-to-day while Lydia is always a season or two ahead with designing new products. The three of them and our warehouse manager work pretty well together."

"Could you imagine each of them increasing their responsibilities permanently?" Bill asked.

"I think to a degree Darren and Carol Ann could, but I have a feeling that they both would look to Lydia for overall direction." Sara's words surprised her as she spoke them. "I may have mentioned that I thought Lydia was a little frustrated lately? It just occurred to me that I think she has been trying to step up this past year and help me and I haven't been paying attention."

"Lydia is already what I would call a 'key' employee. Do you think she could become a more prominent leader at BabyBerry?" Bill asked.

"Maybe, yes, I think she could," Sara said, "At least it's worth considering. Based on our discussion last time, I had already decided that I wanted to meet with her and Darren to discuss plans for increasing sales. I think we could have a little sales bump around this idea of Lydia's to celebrate our 20th anniversary."

Bill smiled, "It sounds like Lydia is thinking ahead, and that's a step in the right direction. Let's take a look at the rest of your list and flesh out a plan."

For the remainder of their meeting, Bill and Sara looked at their "Top Three" Priorities List and crafted some objectives. Sara decided she would have a planning meeting with her key team and have them help create the plan.

"It's not a surprise to them that sales are flat and that I want us to grow. I think in some sense they'll be relieved that we're shifting out of neutral and moving ahead," Sara said. "And it won't be hard for me to talk about needing to be less reliant on key employees and suppliers. We've had a couple supplier failures over the past year. It's not difficult to imagine what would have happened if Kit had still been our chief design person either."

"No, I'm sure it wouldn't be," Bill agreed. "I think you understand what you need to do with BabyBerry. What about you? How are you going to start working on your personal future plans?"

"What do you mean? Don't you think all the business initiatives I have on my plate are enough?" Sara asked.

"I'm afraid that if you only work on the business side, you'll be in exactly the situation we want to avoid," Bill told her. "I want you to add one very small thing to your life this week in each of the three areas that are most important to you personally. Take a step forward to discover your 'cycling.' And it can't just be thinking about it. It needs to be a task or an activity that you can actually do."

Sara was frustrated. The idea of adding one more thing to her task list was overwhelming. "I'm not sure I understand."

"For example, let's take becoming more physically active. I'm not saying you need to go run a marathon or take up hang gliding. But can you squeeze five to ten minutes into each day for a quick walk around your building?" Bill asked. "I'm asking that you take that big idea of something you want to do post-BabyBerry and break it down into a tiny action you can start doing now. This will signal to you and your mind that you're moving forward and embracing the change that is destined to come."

"Now I understand," Sara said. "Baby steps."

"Yes, small steps can add up," Bill said, "but most importantly they'll start changing the way you look at your everyday life and your future. Take a day to think about it, and email me what you're going to do."

Sara left Bill's office knowing what she needed to do with her team. She was excited to get started. Now that they had uncovered the strategy piece, she and Bill would start meeting monthly in addition to email check-ins. The changes that she needed to make in her personal life seemed a little vague, but she knew that with Bill's help, she would work them out.

"I can do anything I want," she said aloud as she looked in the rearview mirror. Sara caught herself smiling, because she knew it was true.

◉ ◉ ◉

- How long could you be away without negatively impacting your business?
- Are there family members or key employees to whom you could transition your business?
- What new activity could you integrate into your life 5-10 minutes per day?

CHAPTER 7

Sara had decided – and Bill had agreed – that she would have an initial meeting with each of her team members before doing any planning. This would allow Sara to follow up on any individual concerns her team might have and allow her to plan more carefully. By the end of the next week, she had met with each of them. Sara thought things had gone well.

As she told Tom later, "I'm pleasantly surprised at how candid everyone has been. Frankly, I think they've been a little worried that the company has been coasting. There were a lot of good ideas, and I think our planning meeting will go well."

"What do you think about Lydia?" Tom asked. "Do you think Bill's hunch is right and she could be the future leader of the company?"

"I think it's possible," Sara answered. "She has a really great grasp of the company and big-picture thinking. I'm not sure if she thinks of herself that way, but it may be because she's always been in Kit's and my shadow. Regardless, she's a key employee and in almost any scenario, a new buyer would want to retain her. She and I both agreed that we needed to shore up her department so that we would always have a backup."

"How did you bring that up?" Tom asked. "I would think it would make people nervous."

"I was pretty straightforward and told everyone that over the past few months I've realized that if Lydia hadn't come on board, BabyBerry would have been at risk with Kit's passing," Sara answered. "I think everyone could understand the possible impact if Lydia wasn't here."

Sara also realized in speaking individually with her team that she had been going through the motions over the past year and not really listening as she should have been. To a certain degree, each team member had been holding back on some of their issues because they didn't want to "bother" her. While she appreciated their concern, she also realized this could have put the company at risk. She vowed to do better and told Tom, "The good news is that I feel ready to tackle everything. I know we'll be stronger."

Sara had decided on a list of personal "baby steps." The list included getting back to the gym three times a week, and she had hired a physical trainer to help keep her promise to herself. She had also decided to spend five minutes each day either looking at property listings online or checking out some renovation blogs and websites. She didn't have to buy, but she could certainly look.

Her third personal list item came via a phone call and an invitation from Dr. Marti Phillips, the CEO of the hospital where Sara sat on the advisory board for the Family Center.

"Marti, how are you?" Sara asked when she heard her voice.

"I'm well, Sara, thank you," Marti answered. "I wanted to check in and let you know the hospital's Board of Directors has an opening and your name has been submitted to fill that vacancy. I typically like to have a conversation with the nominees before we go through the formal nomination process to make sure it's something the nominee is interested in. BabyBerry and your family, and especially you, have been a great friend to the hospital, Sara, and I think you would be a perfect addition to the Board. Your work with the Family Center Advisory Board has been outstanding. I'm not sure we would be as far along without your support."

Sara started to say that she didn't have time, and then she heard Bill's voice telling her she needed to have "a passion for the purpose" in her future. She had always said that when she had more time, she'd volunteer more. Instead she said, "I would love to be considered. What do I need to know about the position, and what are the responsibilities?"

After she hung up the phone she was able to email Bill back with her list. She knew she was starting down the road to a different life, and she was excited.

The day of the team planning meeting, Sara awoke with anticipation and concern. She was thrilled that her team was so supportive, but worried that she was perhaps not ready for the changes that were sure to come. She thought back to the day she had incorporated the company and filed the paperwork with the state. At the time, she knew that if BabyBerry didn't work out, she could go back to being an analyst at the bank after the kids were all enrolled in school. So the risks actually felt small, and she was open to trying new things. Ironically, it was that same attitude she needed now to be successful with this next push.

Her doubts vanished once her team was gathered in their conference room. The excitement was palpable, and she realized she owed her team the best opportunity to make BabyBerry successful. Sara started the meeting by reviewing the sales data that she and Darren had put together. Then she simply re-stated, "We have worked hard, but we've also been fortunate to get the company to this point. What will it take for us to successfully and profitably grow BabyBerry to double our sales in the next five years?"

Sara had shared her mandate when she met with them individually and had asked them to put together an informal "state of their department" presentation for the group. Before they presented, she asked the group to keep their minds open to the possibility that BabyBerry had a bigger position in the world, and it was their job to look for it. They didn't need to worry about the "how," but only the "what" of where they wanted to be. Bill had warned her that focusing on the "how" too early would limit the ideas of her team. She and the company would benefit if she could get buy-in to the future they helped create for the company.

By the time the last person had presented, the conference room had flip chart paper with notes on half of the walls. She gave everyone a break while they waited for the lunches to be delivered. Lydia was the last to leave the room. Sara asked her, "What do you think?"

"Personally, I'm excited," Lydia told her. "I think the others are too. I'm sure there are concerns, but we really do have a committed team here, Sara. I don't know if I ever shared this with you, but I really didn't want to leave L.A. But I told my husband the other night that while I moved here kicking and screaming, I don't think I could have ever found a better opportunity anywhere else."

After everyone had a chance to eat most of their lunch, Sara shared her second planning process objective. "It's obvious to me that all of you put a lot of thought and effort into your updates and your ideas. I'm excited to dig in and start formulating our plan. But before we get started, there's one other element I'd like to include in our thought process that will show we are a success."

Sara paused for a moment. "I've realized that losing my mother last year was not just tough on me and my family, but the BabyBerry family as well. Some of you knew Kit for just a few years, and others helped start this company with us. Someone pointed out to me recently that BabyBerry is at risk because I haven't done a good job of making sure that there is a back-up or succession plan for all the key positions. It was Kit who asked, or maybe demanded, that we look for someone to replace her eight years ago. And because she did that, Lydia has stepped in beautifully to fill that role. Can you imagine the challenges we *could* have faced had that not happened?"

Sara looked around the room and saw people nodding in agreement. "So when we create our plan today, we need to grow the business. But we also need to make sure that we are evaluating and grooming talent from within and determining what we are going to need to do when we double our sales. That includes every position from me throughout the entire company. I don't have an answer right now on exactly how it's going to happen, but I wanted to be clear that this is one of the outcomes I expect."

Sara had asked Char to update the organizational chart, and now she passed it out to everyone. "Moving forward, we will review this chart for changes and additions and to identify areas that need our focus at each monthly team meeting. So, growing our sales, improving profitability, and creating a deep bench of talent – through training or with any new hires – are our three main objectives. Let's start generating our ideas."

They spent the next two hours creating and refining their list. They identified ten new projects that would help them get to their goals. Each manager was assigned at least one project, and then they determined who would be on each project team. By the time they were finished, all the full-time employees were assigned a team. They agreed to spend the next two weeks working on a project plan, including timelines and necessary resources, with their project teams, and that they would each give a report at their next meeting. Sara was visibly excited with what they had come up with, but she saw that her team seemed a little tired and, perhaps, overwhelmed.

Sara wrapped up the meeting. "I know this has been a long day for us, as we're typically not sitting this long on a daily basis. But it's important that I share this with you. I have never been more excited and proud of this company and our team as I am today. Everyone in here participated, had great ideas, and gave good feedback. There is no doubt in my mind that we are going to hit our targets and knock these projects out of the park. I firmly believe that we will look back on this in a year and be amazed at how far we've come."

Before she left for the day, she sent Bill an update from the meeting with a list of the projects and a quick overview of next steps. In the morning, she received this response:

Sara,

Thank you for the update. It sounds very promising and sounds like it went very well. Remember that your goal as 'bicycle builder' is to start handing off the baton and letting others lead.

Your future is beyond the success of these projects!

Best,
Bill

While Sara understood that Bill was trying to keep her focused, she looked at the email and felt slightly deflated. She had been proud of the way her team had pitched in and how she had facilitated the meeting. Bill was speaking as if completing all these projects was a given!

Later that day Sara had lunch at the hospital with Dr. Phillips. Marti Phillips was a firecracker, and Sara had always enjoyed their conversations. After an assistant brought in their lunches and they settled in at Marti's conference table, Marti updated her on the Board. "Your board membership was approved by the Membership Committee. The official vote will be at this month's meeting where you will be introduced. I'm thrilled that you decided to join our little merry band!"

Marti went on to discuss some of the new challenges coming up as well as the new fundraising campaign. "But this is what I really want to discuss with you. We are looking at applying for a five-year grant to expand the capabilities of the Family Center and provide more community education and outreach. You and Tom, along with BabyBerry, have always been such a big supporter of this part of the hospital; I'm wondering if it's a project that you would be interested in co-chairing."

Marti continued to share her vision for the expansion and what it would do for the community. "As you know, families with critically ill children have higher separation and divorce rates. We believe our program is a way to help families cope with the immeasurable stress that comes from these situations. This grant – which I believe we have a high degree of certainty in receiving – will help prove our model on a larger scale. I've approached a few others, like yourself, to be on the committee, but Lee, the Director of the Center, specifically requested that I reach out to you. You've been both pragmatic and strategic on the Center Advisory Board and it's a voice that's needed."

Sara didn't know what to say but she found herself very interested in Marti's proposal. When the twins were born and

Eliza was just two, she and Tom were young but had plenty of family support. They had known others from their time in the NICU whose babies had died or continued to have significant health issues. The stress on the parents was immeasurable, and Sara could see the value that this would bring to the families using the Family Center.

"Marti, I'm flattered," Sara said as she started to decline the opportunity. She then remembered the email she had received from Bill – "your future is beyond these projects" – and continued, "I'm interested, but I would want to be able to make a full commitment to the project if I accept your offer. I'd like to look at my schedule and speak with Lee to learn a little more about her expectations before I make up my mind."

"That's all I can ask, Sara," Marti said as they wrapped up the meeting. "We're looking forward to having you on the Board and hopefully help shepherd the new Family Center project through to fruition. I'll let Lee know to reach out to you."

- Have you identified back-up resources or employees for the key positions in your company?
- How often does your company engage in continuous improvement or special projects to develop new opportunities for your company?
- Is it time to create additional leadership opportunities for you outside of your business?

CHAPTER 8

The next few weeks were busy for Sara. Her team was focused on their new projects, and BabyBerry was in high gear. Additionally, all three of her children made an appearance at the end of their spring break before they went back to campus. On Saturday night they built a bonfire in the backyard fire pit, and the five of them stayed up late in the night. She knew as they graduated from college and pursued their own lives, these gatherings would be less frequent, and she wanted to enjoy every minute. She mentioned that to Tom as they crawled into bed that night.

"I'm sure it's possible, Sara," he answered. "But look at us – we ended up living just a few miles from your parents with you and Kit working together for almost 20 years. I'm sure when you were Eliza's age, you didn't think any of that was going to happen."

Sara drifted to sleep smelling the campfire smoke in her hair, and she didn't even mind. The next morning, she watched the three of them leave to drive back to campus together with a tinge of sadness. A few weeks later, Sara was surprised when she received a text on Tuesday from Eliza saying she would be home that Friday night. She must be getting nervous about graduation, Sara thought.

The plans for the 20th anniversary campaign were starting to come together as well. Lydia and Darren had asked to update her that week. When she walked into the conference room, Sara noticed that easels and story boards were set up all around the room.

Darren and Lydia reviewed the creative designs from the advertising agency with Sara. All three of them had similar feedback; Darren would forward it back to the agency. Lydia reviewed the product development progress, and Darren went over the timeline for advertising, collateral, and website changes. Sara was very pleased. It looked like the October launch would be on time, and just a few weeks later than the anniversary of the actual incorporation date of the company! As Sara was thinking back to that time, Darren and Lydia were throwing knowing glances back and forth.

Finally Sara asked, "Okay, I know both of you well enough to know that there's something else going on. Is there a proverbial shoe waiting to drop that I don't know about?"

Darren looked at Lydia and said, "Lydia and I were approached about an interesting idea and we wanted to show it to you."

Darren got up from his chair and walked to the front of the conference room where a set of story boards were covered on the easel. "In the past, we had discussed opening a local company store and decided against it for several reasons – but primarily because of our longstanding relationship with Rockford's."

Rockford's had been a locally owned department store with several locations in town and across the state. They had been the first retailer to carry BabyBerry bags. Over the years, BabyBerry customers asked for a company store, but Sara and Kit had always felt loyalty to their first retailer, who was just a few blocks away, and had decided against it. As the company's online presence grew, it continued to seem like the right decision to have made.

But Rockford's had closed their last location almost two years ago, and there was no longer a retailer carrying BabyBerry bags in town. Sara and Kit had tossed around the idea of opening a small "pop-up" type store in the neighborhood near BabyBerry shortly afterwards. The neighborhood around BabyBerry had become trendier, with more and more shops dotting the landscape of the old warehouse business. Like many things, Sara had pushed that idea aside after her mother had died.

Darren pulled the cover board away and revealed a rendering of small storefront with the BabyBerry logo. She recognized it as the old leatherworks building across the street. Like many buildings in the neighborhood, it had been converted into loft apartments with retails shops, restaurants, and coffee shops on the ground floor. "I know it was one of the projects that was put on hold, but Lydia and I were approached by someone who wanted to share their vision of what a BabyBerry company store would be and we wanted to show it to you," Darren said.

Darren and Lydia then went through the story boards. Sara was amazed by the level of detail and thought that had gone into the presentation. It was obviously a BabyBerry employee – the look and feel was all BabyBerry. Sara wondered if it was the new designer Lydia had recently hired. After he was done going through the visuals, Darren said, "I went back and looked at our competitors as well as other brands like ours in different spaces. Nearly all of them have at least a small company store. Additionally, I queried the customer service reps and went back through the emails that we get asking about our company store. It's really a lot more than I had suspected. With the additional tourism that has sprung up with the Tech Sector and the University doing so well in their sports programs, there are more and more visitors to town each year. Apparently, there is a 1500-square-foot space opening across the street in June. That home décor store is moving to a larger space down on Main Street."

Lydia chimed in. "At the very least, Sara, I know that you and Kit had discussed a pop-up store, and we were thinking if the price is right, we could do a short lease for the October Anniversary Launch through Christmas," she said. "Apparently, the landlord is open to a short lease if it's BabyBerry."

Sara looked at both Darren and Lydia. She had to admit that the idea was appealing, and she had fallen in love with the designs. But she knew that if they considered doing this, it would need to be a more significant commitment than a holiday pop-up store. Sara was curious and asked, "This is obviously a BabyBerry employee who came up with this idea. There isn't anyone outside of the company who could get this many details right. I'm surprised they aren't here right now – whose idea was this?"

Lydia looked at Darren and drew a breath, "Well, actually, Eliza approached Darren and me about this."

Sara was flabbergasted. Eliza? "What are you talking about? I don't understand."

Lydia chose her words carefully. "Apparently, this was a senior project for her entrepreneurship class. She came by and wanted to get our advice and to make sure that there wasn't anything proprietary about this. And there isn't – she could have easily chosen another company and done the same type of study and presentation."

"I am floored," Sara said, "but I don't understand why she didn't bring it to me."

"I think she wanted to have it graded before she showed it you." Lydia said. "When she brought it to us she was simply looking for feedback before she turned it in. Once we realized this was an idea that should be considered, I decided that the normal protocol was for us to evaluate it and then make a decision to turn it down or promote it to you. We truly believe this is a worthwhile concept and that it should be considered."

The three of them were quiet for a moment. Sara could hear Bill in her head telling her to trust her team and show them how to she'd like them to lead. Both Darren and Lydia knew Sara's children, but the kids hadn't spent an inordinate amount of time at BabyBerry – especially over the last few years. Finally, Sara said, "What do you think are the next steps?"

"I was pretty straight with Eliza. I told her that we saw some potential, and that we'd bring her idea to our meeting for discussion. There were no promises made," Lydia said and then giggled. "I do think it would be fun to see her present this to you."

Sara smiled. "That explains her text saying she was coming home on Friday. Why don't you see if she's 'available' Friday afternoon, and we'll go from there."

On Thursday, Sara and Bill were slated to meet for their monthly check-in meeting. Bill had given Sara a standard format for their meetings. The first hour was a review of results, with the second hour focused on troubleshooting and brainstorming as needed. Sara was to provide updates on both the BabyBerry projects as well as her personal goals. She had also asked him to review the financial statements with her so he could be a sounding board and hold her accountable.

When they finished the agenda, Sara shared the details of her meeting earlier in the week with Darren and Lydia.

"I do think it could be a really fun project to highlight the 20th Anniversary Launch," Sara told him. "But I have to say, I was a little thrown off by the whole thing,"

"That's interesting, Sara," Bill said. "Can you tell me what bothered you the most?"

"I hate to admit it, but I think it's that Eliza went to Lydia first," Sara said.

"I actually think it shows a lot of insight on Eliza's part to not lean on her parent for a favor. It sounds like Lydia and Darren stepped up their leadership," Bill said. "They could have easily dismissed Eliza for fear of what you might say or do. It sounds like they had the company's best interests in mind by making the recommendation. That's not always something easily found."

"I hadn't thought about it that way, but you're right," Sara answered. "It makes me think that considering Lydia for a bigger role in the company is on the right track, and I think we'll need to think about it sooner than later."

She went on to tell Bill about her conversation with Marti Phillips and her request to co-chair the Family Center project. As she wrapped up the project overview for Bill she noticed him smiling and she asked, "Did I say something funny?"

"No," he answered, "I was just noticing how animated you were in talking about this project as well as Eliza's idea for a company store. A purpose and a little passion mixed together, perhaps?"

Sara laughed. "The hospital committee says it would take about ten hours a month, but my guess it would most likely require more of my time, as these things often do. I think about how much it helped our family. How much more could we do for those who don't have the help and resources we did? It feels like something that I am uniquely qualified to do – as a mother and a business owner who serves parents. I emailed the director this morning and let her know that I had accepted."

"So how does that impact your schedule?" Bill asked.

"Our plan was for me to start taking a half a day off per week from BabyBerry," Sara said. "I'm choosing to use that half day to work on outside activities, and this will count as one of those activities. As you suggested, I'm blocking my calendar weekly now to make sure that all the most strategic items are being addressed and letting Char know when there's flexibility and when there isn't. So far it's worked out well. I think I'm a lot less reactive and more productive."

They finished up their conversation. As Bill was leaving he said, "Sara, I've worked with quite a few companies over the years. You really have jumped in with both feet, and I'm looking forward to updating your information in the database in six months. I have a hunch that you'll be surprised at how much your scores will have improved."

"Thank you," Sara responded. "While I didn't realize how stuck I felt, I know now that I think I was really ready to move on. It's been fun to see how ready the employees are in making these changes. We definitely have more ideas than time right now!"

"Possibly so," Bill said, "but that's a good problem to have."

"Yes it is," Sara agreed.

- How often do you and your team review new opportunities to expand your business?
- Do you and your team regularly recognize and celebrate company milestones?
- Does your team have the skills and training to manage projects independent of their day-to-day activities?

CHAPTER 9

Eliza's presentation was scheduled towards the end of the afternoon on Friday. When Sara met Darren and Lydia in the conference room, Sara was happy to see that Eliza was dressed professionally and seemed to be taking the meeting seriously.

Lydia started the meeting off. "Obviously, we all know each other. Eliza, we took some time to share some of your ideas with Sara, your mother…"

Everyone laughed and Lydia went on, "…but we'd like to give you the opportunity to make a formal presentation."

"Lydia, Darren, Sara – thank you for allowing me your time today." Sara smiled at hearing Eliza call her Sara. For many years, Sara had referred to her mother as Kit at work.

It felt too awkward to be calling her Mom in front of the other employees.

When Eliza had been very little, she had scolded Sara for calling her mother Kit. With her little tiny hands on her hips, she had shrieked, "Grams is your MOMMY – not Kit!"

Kit had scooped Eliza up and told her, "Butterbug, your Mommy can call me Swiss Cheese for all I care. I have been her Mommy since the day she was born and I always will be!"

Lydia had told Eliza that she had an hour for the entire presentation. After 50 minutes, Eliza was finished with her formal presentation and asking for questions. They each asked her a few questions and when they were done, Darren and Lydia thanked Eliza and excused themselves.

Eliza sat down next to Sara, "Mom, thank you for letting me do this."

"Oh, honey," Sara sighed, "You did a very good job today, but you really have Lydia and Darren to thank for this. They really went to bat for you. I'm just not sure how this all happened and I didn't know anything about it."

Eliza drew a big breath. "I want to let you know I've been thinking about this for a long time. It was something that I talked to Grams about last year, and she was going to help me talk to you and Dad about this. But then she... well, she's gone and everything changed. I felt kind of stuck."

Eliza stopped for a moment and then went on, "Mom, do you remember at Christmas when Grandpa asked me about graduation and you gave him the evil eye?"

"You noticed that?" Sara asked.

"Mom – everyone noticed. Poor Grandpa! He was just trying to help. He cornered me later and told me that Grams had shared our plan before she died," Eliza explained. "And he encouraged me to go for it."

Sara was confused. Kit and Eliza had a plan? Her father was involved? "Eliza, I talk to your grandfather several times a week and he never mentioned this to me once!"

"I know. I swore him to secrecy because I didn't want him to get in the middle of this," Eliza looked at her straight in the eye, "I want to work at BabyBerry after graduation. I'm not doing this because of Grams or because I'm scared to go out get a job on my own or because I think I'm entitled to the company. This is what happened. The more business classes I started taking, the more I kept thinking about BabyBerry. It got to be where I was obsessed and *everything* applied to BabyBerry! That's when I went to Grams and we had our talk and came up with a plan."

Sara didn't know what to say and so she asked, "A plan?"

"I wanted to show that I was serious. And I thought if Grams thought it was a good idea, she would help me figure it out," Eliza said. "I mean Grams was Grams – she knew everything."

She knew everything. The enormity of that statement hit Sara hard. Eliza must have noticed because she said, "I think Grams wanted us to have the chance to work together the way the two of you worked together. It meant a lot to her – Grandpa told me that too."

Eliza unzipped her portfolio to gather her story boards. "So, this is what Grams said. 'BabyBerry is like your mother's fourth child. What can you do to show her that you deserve a shot to work there and that you're not just asking to be the owner's daughter?'"

"Originally, we had planned to talk to you together last summer, but that never happened. Then for my senior project, I had to take a company and provide a brand and product assessment with a recommendation to enhance the brand. I chose BabyBerry because – why not? Also, because I wanted to show you that I really know the company and that I really care what happens to it. Do you know that less than a third of all businesses make it to the next generation? I guess I want us to be one that makes it."

Sara looked at Eliza and asked, "How did you get all the information?"

Eliza beamed. "Obviously, I couldn't live in this house and not know anything about the company, but I did all the research myself. I felt like it would be cheating if I talked to Lydia or Darren. But then I thought I should at least have them check it over in case I was sharing something I shouldn't. I wanted to prove to you that I could do this on my own. I got an A, by the way."

"Honey, I have to say, I'm shocked," Sara began. "You never showed much interest in BabyBerry before. I'm having some difficulty getting my head around this."

"I know, Mom. Grams said the same thing. I wish I could give you a really logical answer. But this is the best way I can explain it." Eliza looked up. "You and I are very similar, and when I was younger, like in high school, it made me crazy. I just wanted to be myself. I couldn't wait to go to college and figure out who that was. But the longer I was away, the more I realized

I could be like you and still be me. I guess I had to go away to figure that out."

Sara took a minute to choose her words carefully. "Eliza, I'm extremely proud of you for taking the initiative to do this. What are you looking for if you were to come to work at BabyBerry?"

"Honestly, Mom," Eliza said, "I would do anything that you needed from me. I can't sew well enough to work as a crafter but I think I could do just about any other starting job here."

"Eliza, I think there are several things you could do here," Sara said, "but you've been thinking about this for over a year and this week is the first time I've heard about it. I'll meet with Darren and Lydia on Monday, and we'll get back to you when we figure out the next steps. It's my job to make sure this is a good decision for the company as well as for you."

"I know, Mom," Eliza said. "I just hope you give me a chance to prove to you that I really want this and I'm serious."

Sara got up to hug Eliza. "I really am proud of you, sweetie. Now let's head home. I heard a rumor that your Dad was leaving the office early so he could make his favorite daughter her favorite dinner."

Eliza laughed. "He texted me this afternoon with a picture of the chocolate cake he grabbed from the grocery store."

When they arrived home, Tom was with Sara's father on the back deck preparing the grill for the steaks. Sara hugged her father and wagged her finger at him. "So, I hear you were in on this whole thing. How come the mother is the last to know?"

Her father laughed, "I promise, I won't do it again. I felt like I owed it to your mother to see this through."

Sara hugged her father again and helped Tom prepare dinner. They had a nice evening, and Eliza went through the entire story of the project again for Tom's benefit. In the morning, Sara awoke to find Tom downstairs having his coffee and reading a legal brief. She grabbed a cup of coffee and sat across from him. "Eliza still sleeping?"

"No. Your daughter decided that she needed to go for a run. She just left a few minutes ago," he smiled. "How are you doing this morning?"

"Still a little surprised, I think," Sara answered. "I'm not sure what to make of all this. I mean, how serious can she be? She's so young."

Tom smiled. "I think she's pretty serious. She accused me of 'lawyering' her last night after you went to bed when I asked her some questions. You know, you were just slightly older than she is now when we got married, and only a few years older than that when you had Eliza. She reminded me of that last night. Anyway, I don't think she's going to bring it up again this weekend unless you do. She's trying her hardest to prove she's up to the task."

Tom was correct in his assumption. Eliza and Sara went over to shop at the new mall in Smithville in the afternoon. They picked up a few things for the twins and agreed to come home and do some baking. Eliza would drop the care package off at their campus apartment on her way home Sunday morning.

"I hate to rat them out, Mom, but their apartment is a pit. I can't believe they even live like that," Eliza said. "But that's what happens when you get six guys living in one place. I think Matt tried to pick up, but it was a lost cause."

On Sunday morning, Sara hugged Eliza tight and whispered in her ear, "I love you, sweetie. And I'm truly proud of you and thankful you are my daughter. Grams would have been proud too."

Sara felt a lump come up in her throat and Eliza looked away. Tom stepped in, quoting Tom Hanks in *A League of Their Own*. "Okay, you two, there's no crying in baseball, remember?"

"Dad, you are a goof," Eliza said and they all laughed.

Sara told her, "I'll give you a call at the end of the week and we'll talk, okay?"

When Sara met with Lydia and Darren the following week, they both told Sara they were even more convinced that Eliza's idea would be a great opportunity for BabyBerry.

"I know not all brick-and-mortar retail outlets are successful, Sara," Darren said, "But customers have been asking for something like this for years. I also think it will help us get closer to the customer. We can use the information we gather to help us in a number of ways – customer service, product development, and helping the retailers with their merchandising. The question I have is this: is the return on all these things worth the investment? I did some research on some of our retailers who have a similar store footprint to see what their sales are. I think it might be a stretch to for us to make much of a profit with that size store."

Lydia spoke up. "The merchandising tests we could do, though, could help generate more sales overall if we had the ability to test out displays in advance." She looked at Sara. "Do you think we could design the interior space so that we could have our photo shoots over there? If so, it would free up the photo studio space in this building. I know we've discussed leasing more warehouse space for some of the new projects we have coming on line. I keep looking around to see where we're going to expand to."

"That's an excellent idea," Sara said. By the end of their conversation they agreed to move forward with the preliminary budget and plan. "I'll have Tom contact the landlord and see what kind of deal he is looking for."

They agreed to have a follow-up meeting within two weeks. With a targeted soft opening before the 20th Anniversary Launch in October, they were on a short timeframe and would need to make a decision quickly. The new space had very similar "bones" to that of the current BabyBerry building. They agreed it would not be difficult to create the BabyBerry look and feel in the new space.

Sara then added, "Our last topic is hiring Eliza. I'm not going to ask you to make the decision but I would like you to help me understand *if, and where* you think she might add value."

"Sara, Lydia and I discussed this after her presentation last week," Darren answered. "We both agree there is an opportunity for Eliza in each of our departments. I think she would be great working with the retailers and following up with some of the market research that I do."

"I'd like her to help with the merchandising and display info," Lydia said. "She definitely has an eye for it, and, outside of myself, there really isn't anyone else on my team who can do it. Darren and I think we could both keep her more than busy *and* that she'd also be a big help."

Sara looked at both of them. "I think you may have made my oldest child very happy. I'll keep you posted."

Eliza did not disappoint with her enthusiasm when Sara called her to give her the news. "Mom, I promise I will make you so proud. You will not be sorry."

Sara laughed. "Eliza, I have always been proud of you. But I want you to know, if after a reasonable amount of time, BabyBerry turns out to be something that you really don't want to do, I'll understand. Now it's your turn to work hard and go after your own dreams. Not mine or Grams!"

"I know, Mom," Eliza said, "But I am just so excited. So, does this mean the store is a 'go', too?"

Sara told Eliza they were still gathering preliminary information but it looked promising. She explained what Darren and Lydia had proposed. "There are details to still be worked out but it looks like you will split your time working for Darren and Lydia. I might borrow you every once in a while as well. I think I'm going to supervise the store build-out myself."

Eliza was quiet and Sara asked, "Eliza, are you still there. Did I lose you?"

Finally, Eliza said, "Mom, this is so much better than I thought it would turn out. Do you know what I mean?"

"Yes, sweetie, I know exactly what you mean," Sara said quietly and smiled.

- Are you ready for your next big opportunity?
- Do you know which investments in your business will increase the value to an acquirer?
- Are there ideas you have "put on the shelf" that need to be reviewed to grow your business?

EPILOGUE

Sara pulled into her parking space. Today was an important day and she was excited.

As she walked into the building, she looked across the street at the BabyBerry store. She noticed Eliza working on one of the window displays and waved. The store had been open since October and had exceeded their expectations. Eliza waved back and then came across the street to meet Sara.

"Are you ready for the meeting?" she asked her mother.

"Absolutely," Sara answered. "See you at 10?"

"Yes – I'll be there," Eliza answered.

Eliza had worked hard, and the store was a success. Working with Eliza on creating BabyBerry's first retail store had been one of the most rewarding projects Sara had undertaken. She had loved every minute of it – the design of the store, managing the build-out, creating the fixtures, and hiring the staff. Eliza had been at her side the entire way. Working with Darren and Lydia, the four of them pulled off quite the grand opening just in time for BabyBerry's 20th Anniversary Celebration. Like most retail stores, business had slowed in January, but Darren's sales comparisons to other retailers told her team that they were running slightly ahead, and Sara was grateful. They had even received an inquiry from a Property Management Group who owned several upscale shopping malls to discuss expansion to other cities. The first BabyBerry store would most likely not be the last.

As Eliza walked back across the street, Sara couldn't help but reflect on how different she felt. Just a little over a year ago, she had pulled into the same parking place with little enthusiasm for her life and the company she had built. A chance meeting, a reality check, and some help from a trusted advisor, and everything had changed.

Sara shook her head when she thought of the "offer" to buy BabyBerry that had triggered everything. In the end, Sara chose not to sell the company, but she knew she wanted the *ability* to sell the company. In considering her choices she realized that ignoring the inevitable was risking everything she had built. Sara knew now that removing herself from the day-to-day operations of the company was the best gift she could give the company to increase the success of BabyBerry's legacy for years to come. She had never felt so creative and energized, and she realized now that working on future plans for the company was what had always motivated her to do her best work.

Apparently, Pine River Group had been looking at several other companies when they approached BabyBerry. Sara and Darren had attended the Fall Children's Product Show late last year and found out one of their long-time competitors had decided to sell to Goodrich. The owners were about ten years older than Sara and had wanted to retire. The wife had confided in Sara at a cocktail reception that it was proving more difficult than they had imagined to work under the new agreement for someone else. "I'm not sure we'll make it to the end of our agreement," she said. "At this point, I'm hoping for a year."

Sara knew BabyBerry would most likely be sold someday. This process had opened her eyes as well as Tom's, and they decided to have a family meeting with all three children. While neither Matt nor Trevor had expressed any interest in the company, Sara and Tom had thought it important to share their plans for the future. Sara's goals were to ensure BabyBerry would go on long after she was involved with it, and to be fair to the employees who had helped build the company. The choices they would need to make could include transitioning to their children or key employees, or selling to another company.

As part of their process, Sara and Bill kept a list of potential acquirers that supported these choices. Knowing what was important to a buyer would be key in the final decision-making process. Sara had been most concerned about Eliza, since she had been so passionate about working at BabyBerry. She told her daughter, "In the end, regardless of our decision with the company, I want you to have the tools to be successful. If that's at BabyBerry, I'll be thrilled. But I'll be just as thrilled if you're happy somewhere else."

As she walked upstairs to her office, she thought of one of her first, pivotal meetings with Bill McEntire. He had encouraged her to identify activities or passions outside of the company. She had jumped in with both feet as the co-chair of the hospital committee. She enjoyed working with Lee, and their hard work had paid off. Last month, they had received the grant and the next six months would begin the process of staffing and implementing their plan. By the end of the year, her responsibilities with this project would diminish, but Sara was confident she would find a new mountain to climb.

With Bill's encouragement, she and Tom had purchased bicycles. They rode when they had time, exploring the many trails along the river bluffs between here and Smithville. They were planning a weeklong bicycling tour in California's wine country to celebrate their 25th wedding anniversary this summer. She did not, to her husband's sigh of relief, decide to become a "house flipper" and renovate houses. For now, creating the new store and working on the future of the company had satisfied that itch.

Though Fridays were her normal day off, she had decided to have the company meeting today as a way to end the week on a high note. Though she wasn't really concerned, she had cleared her schedule for the rest of the day in case any employees wanted to discuss with her the changes she was announcing.

As they gathered in the lunch room, everyone quieted down when she started to speak. She looked around the room. There were many new faces, but also several that were lifelong employees. She had been thinking of this moment for weeks since they had made the decision and her voice was strong.

"First, I want to thank everyone for a great first quarter. It looks like we will have our best initial quarter ever, and I know it's due to everyone in this room and their hard work. So thank you."

Everyone clapped and Sara went on, "As most of you know, my mother Kit and I started BabyBerry a little over 20 years ago. As a harried mother of three small children, I was beside myself, and my mother's ingenuity helped save me – or at least kept me from going completely bonkers."

Everyone laughed, and Eliza murmured teasingly, "Were we that bad?"

"No, Eliza, you were not," Sara answered. "You were just three children under three years old, and you kept us hopping. From the first bag to the one I saw Eliza putting in the window this morning, it has always been our intent to think of that parent or grandparent who needs that extra pair of hands through a well-made and functional tote. I have never forgotten that first bag that we sold, and I hope BabyBerry carries that passion long into the future."

"So, today, I'm announcing some staffing changes that I'm confident will continue our long tradition of innovation and service. As you know, the new store has been very successful, and we believe there are more untapped opportunities out there for us to explore. In order for me to have the time to explore those opportunities, I will be stepping away from my role as President and into a new role as CEO." Sara smiled and looked around the room. "I am thrilled that Lydia Winchester has graciously agreed to become BabyBerry's next President."

Everyone clapped, and Sara went on to extol Lydia's virtues and some of the other changes. While Lydia would remain

Creative Director, TJ Parrish would now be the Director of Design and Product Development. Darren was now the VP of Sales and Marketing and his assistant, Carey Anne Holloway, was now the Marketing Director. Sara knew they had a few holes to fill, but she was thrilled with the make-up of the team.

As Sara listened to Lydia address the company as President, there was a particular source of pride that she couldn't quite identify. She thought about how Bill had first explained *Tandem Leadership*, and the way she, Lydia, and Darren had worked to implement it over this past year. But now she had switched her role.

"Have you ever watched the Tour de France or any bicycle race?" Bill had asked Sara, "Each team has a lead rider, and it's everyone else's job to help their lead rider be successful. So the other riders deploy tactics and support to make that happen. For example, they estimate that a rider who is following closely or drafting off another rider can save 20% to 40% of their energy. That's why you'll see the other riders on the team take turns in front so that their lead rider can draft off of them and recover some strength. I often think of this strategy when someone like you decides to hand over the reins but is still involved. You are clearing the way so that you, and by default, your team, can be more successful. Not everyone can get there, Sara, but when they do, they often find that they've managed to incorporate their purpose and their passion for the ultimate win."

Sara had asked Char to have some light food and snacks brought in along with some sparkling cider and sodas. She asked everyone to toast Lydia and the entire BabyBerry team, and encouraged everyone to take some time to celebrate. While she had let everyone know that she would be available the rest of the day to answer any questions, those who did stop by wanted to say hello to Sara or let her know their enthusiasm for the changes. Her conversations with both new and long-term employees only strengthened Sara's conviction that she had made a good decision.

Lydia stopped by as Sara was readying to leave for the day and said, "Well, this was a day that I didn't get much work done! I think I've spoken to every single employee!"

Sara laughed, "Welcome to the club! That *is* your job now!"

Lydia nodded in agreement, "You're right. Thank you again, Sara. This is so much more than I could ever imagine have happened when I dropped off my resume nine years ago."

"Thank you, Lydia," Sara answered warmly, "for agreeing to take this on. I couldn't imagine doing this without you."

They chatted for a few more minutes and then Sara prepared to leave for the day. Eliza had organized a family dinner at The Oak in one of the private dining rooms. Matt and Trevor were coming home from college, and Sara's father was joining them, too. As Sara pulled out of the parking lot, she looked at the BabyBerry building in her rearview mirror.

"Thanks, Mom," she whispered, and she drove off to meet her family.

- Spend a few minutes imagining what the "perfect day" would look like at least one year from now:
  a. What would you be doing?
  b. What would you have wanted to accomplish?
  c. How would you feel about your life?
  d. How would you feel about your business?

CONCLUSION

The statistics on the number of businesses that change hands each year are murky at best. Some businesses are sold or transferred in formal transactions. But many others just cease to exist. Their assets are simply liquidated and they close their doors, never to be heard from again. Clearly, some of these businesses owe their fate to poor management and competitive markets. But many have owners that no longer choose to work and have not prepared their business to be sold.

At a recent conference of mergers and acquisitions professionals, business brokers and coaches discussed that business sales and transfer activity appear to be up. While there isn't any single factor responsible for this activity, it's not difficult to imagine the impact that the "Great Recession" and aging ownership has had. Indeed, a small survey of business owners in my network showed there was a strong desire to sell or transfer their business. But, paradoxically, these same business owners had much less of an interest in what actually makes a business more valuable to sell. Perhaps this is where some of the problem lies – what allows a business owner to make a profit or collect a salary cannot always be easily sold or transferred to someone else. And even if it's possible to sell, the proceeds may be much less than the business owner had anticipated.

It is estimated that the entire transition process for a business that is actually *ready* to sell can last anywhere from three to five years. And yet many sellers believe a transaction can take place in less than 12 months. For this reason, regardless of the number of years of business ownership, I now always ask my clients *when* they plan to sell or transfer their business. I have found that many wait much too long to consider the final disposition of what is often their single largest asset. The sooner business succession is addressed and incorporated into the overall strategy of the business, the better chance to sell the business and for the owner to leave the business on his or her own terms.

The most compelling reason to bring on a second-in-command at any phase of your business is twofold. First, it gives you the additional support to systematically put the systems and talent in place to create a business that runs more effectively and ultimately is able to be sold. Secondly, and often more importantly, if you want to be less involved in the day-to-day operations and eventually sell your business, you can then effectively prepare for a successful transition to life after running your business. It is a significant life transition, one whose impact is often underestimated and for which many business owners are ill-prepared. After twenty, thirty or more years in business, this sudden loss of identity can be huge, ultimately making the golden years much less so.

Just as it was never Sara's intention to *not* think about the long-term disposition of her business, many business owners wait to plan for the future until there is a catalytic event or simply an increasing dissatisfaction with their business and their life. Like any relationship that has been neglected or soured, it is heartbreaking to see an owner walk away because he or she waited too long to fix what was broken. I have worked with owners who, like Sara, were sure they were done with their business only to be renewed by a new purpose and appreciation for their life's work. Similarly, there are others who in preparing to sell their business know that completing that transaction is the only outcome that will be acceptable to them. Regardless, *having the choice* is the common element in either situation.

My goal in writing this book is to give you a framework that will allow you that choice. Using this model for successfully anticipating and positioning your business for the future should help you avoid some of the challenges and pitfalls that have befallen those who have gone before you. Many of the strategies used with my clients to set up a company and its ownership for a successful transition are also excellent business management strategies. That is why I often encourage my clients to consider the endgame in their business from the very beginning. Being more profitable and easier to manage makes every business more attractive – regardless of ownership.

For every journey, the only thing we know for sure is that each has a beginning, middle and an end. Making sure your journey ends on your terms will depend on your ability to learn, grow, and adapt to the conditions along the way. I hope that *Changing Lanes* provides you the roadmap to guide you to the freedom you were seeking when you began your journey.

ACKNOWLEDGEMENTS

Thank you to the companies who have given me feedback and support to shape the direction of this book. While there are many, a special thanks to:

- Accretive Strategies
- Ady Advantage
- Blue Rock Search
- Cascade Hypnosis Center
- Diversified Diamond Products
- Harvard Corporation
- Imagehaus
- New North Inc.
- Nanocopoeia, Inc.

- Priorities Group, Inc.
- The Odd Couple Team
- Unlimited Wire Services of Wisconsin, Inc.

Thank you to my editor, Maggie McReynolds, Jenn McRobbie, Vice President, and the entire Difference Press team for making this such an amazing process.

Thank you to Angela Lauria, Publisher, Difference Press, for knowing that I could write another book. Your insight and guidance has been invaluable and appreciate all you have done more than you will ever know.

To the Morgan James Publishing team: Special thanks to David Hancock, CEO & Founder for believing in me and my message. To my Author Relations Manager, Megan Malone, thanks for making the process seamless and easy. Many more thanks to everyone else, but especially Jim Howard, Bethany Marshall, and Nickcole Watkins.

Thank you to Russ – my compass and my rock. With you I have always done more than I could have ever imagined. This book is for you.

ABOUT THE AUTHOR

 Gina Catalano is the founder of Venture Solutions, a consulting and coaching company focused on the success of small companies and their leaders. With over 20 years of experience leading and working with businesses, she has authored the Amazon Kindle bestseller *Tandem Leadership: How Your #2 Can Make You #1.*

In this book she outlines an innovative strategy for entrepreneurs to work with the #2 or "second in command" leader in their company to achieve success in all areas of their lives.

She has worked as a director of consulting for manufacturing companies in addition to stints as a general manager and vice president in entrepreneurial companies. She has been fortunate to work with some of the most dedicated professionals and amazing clients who taught her that pursuing excellence, living your passion, and enjoying your life are not mutually exclusive.

She is a Martha Beck-trained Life Coach and a certified Advisor for the Value Builder System™ based on John Warrillow's book *Built to Sell*. She holds a B.A. in Mathematics from the University of California, Santa Barbara and Masters of Public Administration from California State University.

THANK YOU!

Thank you for reading *Changing Lanes: The Owner's Guide to a Successful Exit*. It's never too soon to plan for your future and the successful transition of your business. After all, isn't that what you've worked so hard for?

If you would like to learn how to implement *Tandem Leadership* in your company, please visit www.venturesolutionsus. com/changinglanes. There you will find a free *Changing Lanes* Toolkit that includes:

- **Free Book** – Receive a copy of my Amazon bestseller *Tandem Leadership: How Your #2 Can Make you #1*
- **Rules of the Road** – A helpful checklist on how to avoid "flat tires" on your road to success with *Tandem Leadership*.
- **5 Keys to Implementing Tandem Leadership** – A bonus audio on *Tandem Leadership* and how to get started.

Keep Riding!

Morgan James
Speakers Group

We connect Morgan James published
authors with live and online events
and audiences who will benefit
from their expertise.

Morgan James makes all of our titles available
through the Library for All Charity Organization.

www.LibraryForAll.org

9 781683 506317